Buildings, Projects, and Babies

Managing to Deliver

**Yasser Osman Ph.D., PMP. &
Yara Osman**

ISBN: 978-1-970024-35-7

Table of Contents

Table of Contents iii

Chapter One: This Is a Book Written for Project Managers 1

Chapter Two: A Healthy Baby Always Comes First 15

Chapter Three: Learning from Amsterdam and Airliners 31

Chapter Four: When the Project Must Be Completed on Time,
No Matter What 45

Chapter Five: Always Test before You Build 59

Chapter Six: It's Academic—Creative Ideas from the
Project Teams of Tomorrow 73

Chapter Seven: Conclusion 91

Project Review Check List 97

About the Authors 105

Chapter One
This Is a Book Written for
Project Managers

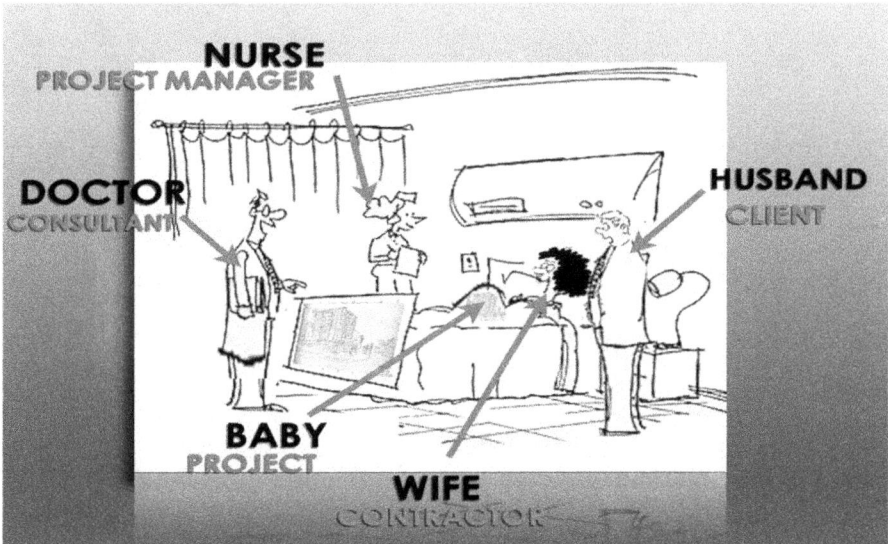

Illustration: An introduction to the main characters of a delivery room and their equivalents in a construction project.

Chapter One

This Is a Book Written for Project Managers

For many years, I have been a project manager for large international construction projects—luxury hotels, brand-new residential communities, shopping malls, even summer palaces for royal families seeking a break from their governing responsibilities. The teams with which I have worked are often as large and complex as the new buildings themselves. Sometimes there are thousands of construction workers on site; countless others transport materials and finished components to the site. Also contributing to the project, although they are never seen, are the employees of factories who manufacture these components.

The process of designing, planning, and managing the actual construction of these buildings is unique in every case, but when you step back there is a certain rhythm that can be found in each, and a consistent cast of characters that while the individuals may change, they always play familiar roles. Even the issues that appear suddenly and create turmoil on site become familiar over time; they are an unavoidable part of the challenge, the excitement, and the rewards of construction project management.

In addition to being an experienced project manager, I am also an architect. I have found that all my skills and education are important assets in keeping projects on schedule, within budget, and in compliance with quality and performance standards. As we will discuss later, it's not that I impose my design skills when managing a project; if I did, I might seek only to propose the "best" solution for issues arising during a project's lifetime, rather than supporting team members whom I hired for their expertise in specialty fields like structural or mechanical engineering. A successful project manager's primary role is to build and maintain a successful *team*, which sometimes means taking a step back from your field of expertise to maintain a team's culture of collaboration and mutual trust and help everyone think outside the box.

Instead, I use my academic background and design experience as a foundation for communication with other members of the project team, and also as a way of assessing potential team members during the critical early stages of a new project. I have found that hiring the right people can make the difference between a successful and (relatively) stress-free project vs. one that is full of turmoil and failure. The ability to engage in an informed conversation with other members of a large construction project team is perhaps the most important first step in successful project management. To be honest, when I graduated I never thought my architectural degree would be so valuable in such an unexpected way.

But because I went on to earn a PhD in architecture from the University of Pennsylvania in 2001, I also bring an academic perspective to my work in project management. I seek patterns and look for analogies to create a larger story from the series of different construction projects that make up my career. And I believe in the importance of sharing these stories with younger future professionals who will carry forward in the field, to help them become successful as individuals, and to help ensure that their projects will meet the ever-increasing demands for cost control, quality, and on-time performance.

So I have decided to write this book, to both summarize the larger lessons that can be learned from a lifetime of experience, and to describe some of these specific experiences so they can tell their own stories to readers.

Whether I ever find the time to become a professor in a design school (and I think not at the present time), I can still achieve some of my goals for educating future professionals in my field by sharing with you, in this book, much of what I have learned.

Why "Buildings and Babies"?

It shouldn't be surprising that as a project manager, I frequently think of the buildings we are constructing as "my babies." They begin as theoretical beings, potential realities drawn on paper, waiting to grow and be assembled. The creative process involved in any number of human endeavors—whether they are the construction of a building, the writing of a book, or the launching of a new consumer product—is often described as "like giving birth to a baby." I am not the first person to use this analogy to describe something new that I am bringing into the world.

But what is new in the case of this book is the extent to which I have expanded this analogy to both people and place. I have used it to describe the various roles key members of the project team play in the construction of a building, along with the idea that the construction site itself be thought of as a kind of "delivery room" where these characters interact.

The people analogies, broadly defined, include the architect or designer, who is most like the doctor in the delivery room, bringing theoretical expertise about how the building "should be" as it is constructed. There is the client or owner, who is most like the father in the delivery room, deeply concerned about the building that will become part of his "family" in the sense that it will become an operating hotel, shopping mall, or residential community. Then there is the contractor, who is most like the mother, who essentially does all the work, is closest to the building or baby, and has perhaps the most at risk during the construction project itself. All these individuals have their own relationship with the building or baby which, until it is completed, cannot speak for itself, but must be represented in project planning and management as interpreted by one or more of the other characters.

And finally there is the project manager, who is most like the nurse in a delivery room. This professional has technical skills and know-how that are like the designer/doctor, but must adjust the application of these skills to the realities of the project as he or she develops and changes with every day on site (that is, in the "delivery room"). Nurses can see newborns as "their babies" in the sense that they share responsibilities for their safe arrival into the world, although they don't have the same history of relating to them as do the father, mother, and doctor, or in the case of a project being constructed, the owner, contractor, and designer. Nurses are closer to mothers during critical times in the delivery room than anyone else, in their ability to monitor events and identify issues that require immediate solutions, find those solutions, and implement them; the same goes for the project manager and contractor. In both cases, the actions of these two characters can be the most important steps toward success or failure at the critical moments when the baby is in the delivery room, or the project is being constructed. When all goes smoothly, they are part of the overall team, ensuring that everything is going according to plan. But when an issue arises, it is the nurse's (project manager's) responsibility to find a solution, create a plan of action that will implement that solution, and rally the rest of the team to agree on a plan and move forward.

Caveat: What the Building and Babies Analogy Is *NOT*

In addition to drawing from personal experience with many construction projects to create an analogy as a learning tool for professionals in my field, I have also chosen the "building and babies" analogy to grab your attention and make you curious. Many people, including my wife, have raised strong objections to the analogy when I first described it to them. "Yasser, what are you thinking?" is what they often say. "Are you saying the designer/doctor is a stand-in for God, the ultimate Designer of a human being?" Many women will add, "And don't you think that both the mother and father have a similar relationship with the baby? After all, in the twenty-first century, parents share in the responsibilities of work and raising children; the father isn't the sole 'owner' anymore." I could go on with other objections, but these are the two most common ones.

My answer is that the analogy is a powerful teaching tool, yet quite limited in the way it should be interpreted. It only works in the delivery room, not during the entire pregnancy. It is during these hours or (God forbid) days that the characters attending to the birth of a baby gather and interact with one other in real time. That is when—and only when—my analogy applies. The analogy doesn't apply to the relationship between the father/client and mother/contractor outside of this time when the medical aspects of the birth process take precedence. The designer/doctor is not God; this character is in the delivery room only as an expert in the medical procedures to follow once a mother goes into labor. And the analogy of the father/client as the only owner of the building/baby is not perfect.

In reality, in today's world both parents often share the role I have created for the father alone, but remember this is a book about construction project management, not maternity ward management. And trust me, the analogy of a nervous father (the client, or owner) in a delivery room, along with the doctor (design consultant), nurse (project manager), and mother (contractor) while a baby (building) is being born works *perfectly* in that direction, even if it raises objections from people who rightly argue that it doesn't work in reverse.

If I were a nurse or doctor, I would never have written a book using the construction of a luxury hotel complex as an analogy to teach medical professionals how to manage a delivery room. The analogy fails in that direction and has no teaching value. But I have often seen clients, designers, and contractors argue about who is to blame when unforeseen critical issues arise on a construction site. Based on this, I believe the analogy of these characters being the father, doctor, and mother in a delivery room is a useful way to capture the need for a calm, creative, and caring professional to serve as the nurse/project manager. This professional is the only one whose job it is to focus on the baby/building and move forward toward a successful outcome, instead of looking for someone to blame. The nurse/project manager must find a path to success, and then bring the others together as a team to find and implement a solution to any issues. If you are a project manager with similar experiences to mine, perhaps you can see this analogy as well as I can. If not, and if I have done a good job of sharing my knowledge, by the time you've finished this book you'll agree with me about the value of my "buildings and babies" analogy.

The Role of the Project Manager

As noted above, it's THE PROJECT MANAGER (or nurse) who is responsible for making sure everyone on a construction project, or in the delivery room, is working together to complete the building, or ensure the birth of a healthy baby. The other characters all have the same interest, of course, but unlike the project manager or nurse, they each have a "safe place" where they can argue for a solution that protects their self-interests along with the health of the baby. The designer can blame the contractor for not following instructions and specifications in the design documents. The contractor can complain that these were too vague to be useful, and then demand a change order to increase his or her payments or extend the project schedule to mitigate risks in adjusting to the new requirements of any proposed solution. The client can, like an expectant father, make emotional demands for answers or threaten vague financial consequences if an issue arises and no solution is implemented, while contributing relatively little of value in times of crisis.

But the project manager has no such safe place. When an issue arises, he or she can only assess the situation, look for a solution, and when that solution is found, start solving the equally difficult matter of getting the rest of the team to agree on how to implement that solution. That is the aspect of project management I want to teach here. It requires both technical and managerial skills—technical in the sense that a real and sometimes complex solution must be found, tested, and verified as a first step in solving issues, and managerial in that this promising solution must then be "sold" to the rest of the team. The next few chapters will illustrate several real-life case studies, showing how this same basic issue can appear in different aspects of a construction project, and how these differences may require outside experts to find a solution and then require political skills in finding other team members to support the solution and convince the others to adopt it.

Readers may note that I've purposefully used the word "issue" instead of "problem" to describe unforeseen difficulties that arise during the lifespan of a typical construction project. This is something I have done on purpose. I never use the word "problem" on a job site or in meetings with team members, because a "problem" is a dead end. It represents a situation without a solution and, in my experience, is always used by those who are not looking for solutions, but rather are resigned to one of two eventualities: they are either identifying a "problem" they expect someone else to solve without their help, or they are determined to accepting the "problem" as being insurmountable and seeking ways to blame others.

I never let team members tell me there is a "problem" during a project unless it is something that cannot be solved. For example, if God forbid one of the contractor's construction workers is killed in an on-site accident, there is certainly a "problem." Nothing can be done to bring that poor individual back to life. To me, this is the only type of event that I will accept as a "problem." Everything else is an issue or a challenge that can be solved, because there is always a solution if professionals put their minds together to find it. But there is also a second part of my team management philosophy that follows from my refusal to allow the word "problem" on a job site. It is the requirement that anyone who brings an issue to the team's attention must also bring a possible solution, or at least help find a solution as a team. Simply identifying an issue and not being willing to engage in finding a solution is unacceptable.

To support this philosophy, sometimes the project manager must consider the professional responsibilities of other team members in the search for successful solutions. The coming pages will include examples of project managers who manage their team to find solutions that are within the professional responsibilities of *one* of the existing team's members—perhaps the contractor or design consultant, for example.

There are also other examples where a successful project manager recruits experts from professions whose areas of expertise are beyond the skills of the original project team. These might include botanists who have discovered ways to manage landscaping techniques that conserve water, or designers of wastewater systems that ingeniously limit their requirement for clean or "sweet" water. Other examples will show novel ways of convincing team members that a promising solution will in fact work, or fitting these solutions into a plan that doesn't upset the balance of responsibilities and liability risks of team members (as defined in their original contractual arrangements). There are no limits to the creativity, professional skills, and managerial expertise required to solve issues that arise in today's construction industry.

A Few Helpful Hints for Today's Project Managers

In my experience, there are a few broad lessons to remember in approaching the unique issues that will arise in every new project. Here are a few, in summary, to help you recognize elements of the case studies that follow in this book, and to remember in your work as a successful project manager.

1. **The importance of a "matrix" team structure and how project team members relate to each other.** Over the years, I have worked on projects that practiced a traditional vertical (or *hierarchical*) management team structure, and on others using a matrix, allowing for both vertical management and horizontal communication among team members across organizational lines with similar responsibilities and skills. The results I have seen in problem-solving abilities have favored teams with a matrix structure. Vertical management structures keep lines of authority clear, which is reassuring for project teams where the importance of maintaining lines of responsibility and strict maintenance of existing liability agreements are important. But these structures do little to solve complicated issues and sometimes do nothing more than influence the settlement of lawsuits once issues become problems that have done irreparable damage to a project, forcing a failure and resulting legal proceedings. Strong matrix team structures, on the other hand, allow people with similar skills from different organizations to work together to match issues with successful solutions, and thereby unleash the creative brain power available within the team to overcome barriers to success. The strong matrix structure is much preferred in my opinion; it creates trust among team members, and this trust can be extended to support even more creative solutions by engaging outside experts or employing innovative project management methods (such as demonstrations of proposed solutions to create consensus for new and successful solutions).

2. **Remember the factors that are most important for success in the project.** We all know the "big three" in this category: money, time, and quality. Money is another term for the project budget, and time is of course directly related to the project schedule. Quality is often expressed in terms of durability of materials, performance of systems, and the look and feel of interior finishes, exterior surfaces, and landscaping. When issues arise, a project manager can find the quickest and best path toward a solution in some cases by identifying which of these factors is most affected and then engaging those team members with the most to gain or lose if an issue becomes a problem.

   For example, if the project schedule is affected and it absolutely positively has to be completed in order for the client to succeed, the project manager might find an ally in the client for promoting a solution to other team members. Project managers might also consider remembering the increasing importance of environmental factors in the future, and look toward solutions that save natural resources like water, recycle waste materials, or reduce a project's carbon footprint in other ways like reducing the need for long-distance shipping of materials and components (more on each of these later).

3. **Not all project team members are created equal.** In some cases, such as projects in which the owner or client is a large organization like a government agency, there is no identifiable initial decision-maker. This is important because, unlike a smaller project like an individually owned and operated hotel, it will be difficult to find someone who can represent the owner in problem-solving decisions. An individual hotel owner will have specific priorities when it comes to a total budget, a project schedule, or relevant quality concerns. But a large organization will only have employees, none of whom will want to assume the risk of changing anything that might jeopardize their career paths. The absence of an initial decision-maker can be a serious concern in and of itself when issues arise, since the project manager will need to depend on other team members to study, develop, and advocate for

solutions. A large client will almost always be the last to sign onto these changes and will probably only do so when it is clear there is absolutely no risk involved at all. This makes it important to plan the project with extreme care and attention to all possible issues so they can be addressed and solved before they become large enough to involve the large organizational owner.

4. **Think broadly about learning**. There are a few points to make on this subject. First, remember your favorite maxims from school. Mine is "fail to plan = plan to fail." The importance of this can be seen in the above example about needing to be careful when working for a large organizational owner. Anticipating issues is always critical, but more urgent when a project manager knows the opportunities to find willing problem-solving partners will be rare. Failing to plan in these cases truly raises the risk of planning to fail. Another of my favorite lessons is to be willing to unlearn some long-held beliefs to solve new issues. I've often reminded other team members of this need, particularly when an approved construction process has proven to be ineffective due to unanticipated issues, yet no one seems to want to try anything new. Success or failure sometimes rides on the project team's willingness to move forward with a new approach, and it's up to the project manager to find it, test it, sell it, and implement it. Therefore, being willing to learn something new is the main responsibility of the project manager. The third and final learning-related point I'd like to make is always to remain *committed to learning*, not only when looking for new solutions, but also when the project manager needs to convince team members of the value of a new and creative solution. Sometimes demonstrating the likely success of a proposed solution is the best way to build a consensus for implementing it. I'm a firm believer in demonstrations of new ideas and the use of mock-ups to test materials or different construction methods. Allowing other team members to learn by doing is a great way to build and maintain a strong team. Seeing is believing, and whenever possible, build slack time into the project schedule to allow for demonstrations and mock-ups; they are a

great way to solve many issues that threaten the success of a project.

5. **Select team members for competence and commitment**. The first few months of a project schedule are the most important. This is not only because it is a time to anticipate possible issues and brainstorm ways to minimize their likelihood or solve them if they arise. It is also because this is when a project manager hires the team that will help keep things on track. My strong recommendation for project managers is this: hire people who have stronger skills than you have in *their* area of expertise. Hiring people who don't know as much as you is tempting because it allows you to keep control, but it doesn't help solve an issue that's beyond your capabilities. And, when it comes to the two parameters of competence and commitment, other than the obvious observation that it's best to hire someone with both, what are the relative merits of the other combinations? I'm glad you asked…

If you hire younger individuals, it's best to look for commitment, since they'll learn competence over time. When it comes to the *worst* possible combinations, however, the answer might surprise you. Most people think someone with neither commitment nor competence is the worst, but in fact, in my experience, that's the second-worst combination of qualities in an employee. The worst is someone competent *but not committed*. These individuals are likely to lag in applying their skills in productive ways, but because they are skilled, they will second-guess solutions and blame others for failures that could have been prevented if they had found a solution. People who are competent but not committed don't care, and they run the risk of being corrupted and engaging in other destructive behaviors, such as taking advantage of their position for their own personal gain at the expense of the project. Beware of those who are competent but not committed!

6. **Never be afraid of wrong decisions made with good intentions**. Wrong decisions can be damaging but, on the other hand, everyone

makes mistakes. When managing people with good intentions, it's important to allow them to learn from their mistakes. Inform them of their mistakes and the consequences, but be sure to provide for learning opportunities. In fact, whenever possible, ask for their ideas about correcting their mistakes. It will foster a sense of relying on themselves for finding creative solutions, and will also encourage them to take responsibility for future decisions, even after they've made a mistake that might otherwise discourage independent thinking. I often look at mistakes made with good intentions as ideas that were valid, except that they were made with incomplete knowledge of the situation at hand. Instead of giving my team the impression that I'm looking for someone to blame when mistakes occur, I always want them to know I'm looking for solutions. This keeps everyone—even the team member who made the original mistake—involved in being part of the team.

Chapter Conclusion: The Three Certainties of Project Management

The successful birth of a new baby in the delivery room and the efficient completion of a construction project require collaboration and coordination among all team members. It is the project manager's responsibility to make sure this collaboration and coordination is maintained on site, and to bring the team back together when they need help working together.

Regardless of the application of my "buildings and babies" analogy, or the different types of challenges that await project managers and the skills required to meet them, project managers and those who love them must remember these three certainties about the profession:

1. **There will be issues**. This is an unavoidable aspect of every project that will ever be managed. An effective project manager will always be ready for them, whether he or she identifies them first, or if they are brought to the project manager's attention by another team member.

2. **There are no problems, only issues with solutions**: Remember to keep the team focused on problem solving, not simply identifying problems. Use my example of a "problem" as being a situation where there is no possible solution. A successful project manager, and a successful project team, refuses to accept this conclusion and instead focuses its time, energy, and creativity on the search for solutions and the implementation of a solution that works. Note that in subsequent chapters, in the interest of using common English, I will resume using the word "problem" to talk about issues that arise in construction projects that require solutions. This in no way undermines my commitment to banning the word "problem" from your project management philosophy and all conversations with members of your team, and we will revisit this important matter again in the conclusion of this book.

3. **The project manager is responsible for solving issues, but only to the extent that he or she can tap into the expertise, creativity, and commitment of the project team.** Solutions come from collaboration and positive thinking by the entire team, not from any single individual. Managing a successful team that identifies issues and ways to solve them is what we do and why we exist.

Chapter Two
A Healthy Baby Always Comes First

Illustration: Supplier schematic of fiber cement board wall system, showing the walls in place and describing benefits in terms of cost, schedule, and quality.

Chapter Two
A Healthy Baby Always Comes First

In this example, the characters in the construction project "Delivery Room" are forced to solve an issue in which the health of the project/baby is seriously threatened. While the collaboration of all parties is required to solve a life-threatening issue like the one we will explore, that collaboration is absent long enough to require one of the characters to seek a solution on their own. The project is ultimately saved not by an agreement among all the parties to seek a solution as a team, but by this single character's successful discovery of a solution outside of the delivery room. The other characters remain stuck in nonproductive demands for a solution by someone else, and with a search for blame instead of a good answer for how to save the health of the project/baby.

Collaboration eventually returns to the delivery room, and a healthy project/baby is delivered on time and within budget, but because only one of the team members put the project/baby first, it is a collaboration that accepts and implements a solution instead of collaboration among team members to seek and find a solution together. When delivery room teams are rescued by the focus and dedication of a single member, there is essentially no team. In this example, the team's only value is an object lesson in how not to behave in a time of crisis, so that we can learn from their mistakes. Projects and babies are too precious to leave their health up to the creative contributions of a single team member.

The Situation: A Residential Project and Its Poorly-Timed Boundary Walls

Our project is a major residential development on the outskirts of a large city, comprising more than one hundred thousand square meters of land and the construction of fifty villas and fifteen buildings, and support facilities the new residents of this community would expect. In all, three hundred residential units are planned, representing not only a sizable investment for the client/father, but also the opportunity for significant profit on the sale of these units. All is proceeding according to schedule, perhaps even a little ahead of schedule, and costs are well within forecasts of expenditures to date. The villas are nearing completion and, according to the planning consultant's (in our delivery room analogy, the "doctor's") construction guidelines, it is time to build the boundary walls around the development and similar walls separating the individual buildings (to create privacy). The project manager (in our analogy, the "nurse") calls what is expected to be another routine planning meeting with the managers of the contractor (the "mother" in the delivery room) to begin excavations for the walls, only to find a shockingly serious problem in the proposed construction timeline, one that the project manager/nurse realizes could destroy the project's financial viability with massive cost overruns and schedule delays. The owner (or "father"), ultimately the one whose financial health is most directly affected, was paying close attention, waiting for one of the team's members to propose a successful solution.

The issue is one that could have been avoided with better planning. There was no unanticipated event; for example, no one discovered the ruins of an ancient civilization beneath the surface, there was no toxic waste in soil samples, and there wasn't a strike at the company that produced the slabs and other materials. Instead, the issue was a simple error in timing the construction of the project's individual components. Because the buildings were constructed before the walls, the contractor reported to the project manager that there would be no way to build the walls separating the villas from each other, nor some of the boundary walls. There was simply not enough room between the nearly-complete villas to bring in the construction equipment required to construct the walls! Without a better solution, the villas would need to be destroyed to construct the walls as they were specified in the construction documents, an "answer" that would obviously destroy the profitability of the entire development and perhaps bankrupt the client/father.

It was a shocking issue, not only because of its potential to devastate the project's construction schedule, but because it could easily have been avoided. And this fact—that the life of the project/baby itself was threatened by simple human error on the part of a delivery room team member—caused an uproar at the planning meeting where the project manager announced it. Like a horror-movie version of the stages of grief, that meeting saw team members go from shock and disbelief to a search for blame and demands that someone find a solution. These heated arguments did nothing to solve the issue, of course, and, for a time, not only was the life of the project/baby at risk, but so was the survival of the entire delivery room team.

The synergy of the combined brain power of several talented and skilled professionals is a reason why the construction project/delivery room team can solve many issues that inevitably occur in a project's/baby's construction. But this collaboration only occurs when members of the team form an alliance to search for a solution, find it, and implement it together. This example demonstrates the consequences when emotions lead to conflict instead of cooperation, and when demands for finding fault replace a focus on creative issue-solving.

In situations like this, who can be counted on to take the reins and find a solution on their own? When collaboration isn't possible but an answer is critical to the health of the project/baby, only individual action can save it. The hero, as we will discover, is the project manager. When I describe this situation to my friends and colleagues in the industry, many of them tell me, "Of course, the project manager is the obvious team member to solve this sort of issue, because they are the one professional with access to all other team members and to the best real-time information about the project itself."

But while this is certainly good insight into the role a project manager can play in solving difficult issues, there is another, perhaps even more important reason why this team member solved the boundary wall issue. The project manager was the only delivery room team member able to keep a cool head and look for a solution, instead of joining everyone in the screaming matches that replaced routine meetings for several weeks of the project schedule.

The Issue: Timing Is Everything—Or Is It?

The issue as it was initially discovered in that fateful meeting between the contractor and the project manager was correctly diagnosed as a scheduling error. If only the timing for excavating the foundations required for the boundary walls had been coordinated with the excavation of the buildings themselves, the entire project could have proceeded as envisioned by the planning consultant, and would likely have come in on schedule and under budget. But though this diagnosis was correct—indeed, a scheduling issue caused this issue, one that could have become a life-threatening problem—the solution could no longer involve the project schedule. It was too late, and the costs of destroying already-constructed villas to allow for the as-designed walls to be built were prohibitive.

Who was to blame? The answer isn't clear, because the issue seems to have arisen from an oversight more than an actual error. The plans produced by the consultant didn't specify when the walls should be constructed, only how, and with what materials. The contractor saw this lack of specifications to be the responsibility of the planning consultant, but the consultant blamed the contractor's lack of professional experience as the real cause of the issue. Any contractor who had successfully built a similar development would surely know that all foundations needed to be excavated at a time when heavy equipment could be maneuvered throughout the site; the consultant/planner shouldn't have to think about these sorts of details, they argued.

For a time, both of these team members actually argued that the project manager should have seen this issue coming in pre-project planning based on their experience with other developments, which didn't contribute anything to the search for a solution either. And the client/father could simply observe in disbelief and anger, realizing that if nobody found an answer for this crisis, the project/baby would not survive, and they would face financial ruin. The project/baby, of course, can never speak for itself, leaving the project manager with a choice: either join in the animated and completely unproductive blame game, or look for a solution. Luckily, they chose the second option.

The Solution: Can New Materials Save the Project/Baby?

It wasn't easy. There were continued distractions, with hectic new "emergency" meetings added to the project's regular project meeting schedule. "This isn't my responsibility!" the contractor would argue (and they were correct, of course). "You should have known to dig all the foundations at the same time, given how close the buildings are to the walls in my design documents!" the planning consultant would shout (and they were correct in their own way as well). "I don't care who is responsible, I demand that you solve this problem (he didn't care about my rule and used this word) and deliver a successful project/baby or else!" the client/father would scream (and his frustration could also be easily understood). The possible consequences of what the client/father might do to make good on these "or else" threats could injure or possibly kill either the contractor or the planning consultant, or both—along with the project/baby, of course.

In the middle of this mayhem, the project manager knew there were two possible answers: either destroy the minimum number of already-constructed buildings to construct the walls as shown in the original documents, or look for a new solution. The first option would have perhaps saved some money and time, but not enough to save the project/baby. And so, in the relative peace and quiet between shouting matches, they looked at the issue in a new way. They saw it as an issue not rooted in the project schedule, but in the materials specified for the boundary walls themselves. They looked for a way to build walls that would look and function in ways similar to the ones specified in the construction documents, but which could be built with methods and equipment that would leave the new villas intact.

So they went back to the original documents and found troubling specifications that would require heavy equipment that couldn't fit into the tight spaces between the villas and other buildings. The walls were designed to be made of precast prefabricated concrete, an excellent choice in terms of strength and durability, but a choice that came with the need for substantial foundations requiring excavations deep and wide enough to require heavy equipment: two and a half meters deep and two meters wide. The first alternative answer was to find another way to dig these trenches. With lighter construction machinery? By hand? There turned out to be no good answer—the land was rocky and both alternatives would lengthen the schedule and increase costs beyond the limits of what the client/father would accept. A different answer would have to be required, and time was not only running out, it was being consumed by increasingly difficult arguments in the delivery room.

What about different, lighter materials for the wall? Could this be a way to salvage the project? The project manager began looking at other options, bringing the design documents to suppliers who might specify something that would preserve the look, strength, and performance of the original walls while not requiring the same deep and wide foundations that threatened the project's survival. It was a creative idea, although at first there was no guarantee a solution was out there. But, as it turned out, one of the suppliers the project manager knew proposed something promising: fiber cement board. Walls made of this material would maintain the look and performance of the originally specified walls, but would do so at a fraction of the cost and expense. The foundations would only need excavations that were sixty centimeters deep and fifty centimeters wide, a little more than one-quarter of the excavations at the heart of all the arguments in the delivery room. Plus the costs of this solution would actually be *lower* than the original precast prefabricated concrete walls. The project manager was skeptical at first, and did their own checking with colleagues outside of the delivery room team to make sure this wasn't simply a new supplier's sales pitch and not a viable solution to the issue, but this investigation convinced the project manager that lighter fiber cement board walls would save the day. But now that they believed they had a solution, how could they convince the other characters in the delivery room to accept it and move forward with the project? A team that seemed more likely to be resigned to failure and concerned about how to assign the blame for that failure would have to be convinced that success was possible, and then that there was in fact a good solution. The project manager knew they couldn't turn the team around by themselves. They would need an ally.

Success Step One: Finding an Ally to Support a Solution

Once the project manager was convinced that the supplier's solution would work, they looked for an ally in gaining support from the rest of the delivery room team. But who could that be? Depending on the client/father to be that ally was out of the question; they were far too emotional and had lost trust in the other team members. Since the client/father had no technical knowledge of construction materials or methods, they couldn't participate in a rational evaluation of this solution. If they hadn't lost their trust in the other team members, they could have conceivably been approached to continue investing time and money in the project while a solution was found, but it was already too late. The client/father was usually the first to begin screaming in delivery room meetings, so it wasn't feasible to start with them.

What about the planning consultant? They might know more about the new materials, and were certainly motivated to find a solution to save the project and avoid having their reputation damaged, but the project manager wasn't sure about whether they would agree to the use of materials that were different from the ones specified in their original design documents. And even if they knew the fiber cement board was an acceptable substitute, they might be put in the position of having to explain to the client/father why they hadn't specified this better alternative in the first place. It was too risky. If the project manager tried to enlist the support of the planning consultant and failed, the result would be a new argument between these two team members, and the planning consultant might prevail. That would cost the project manager credibility and there would be no one able to propose an alternative solution. There would be too much momentum toward failure for anything else to be a likely outcome.

That left the contractor as the last—and as it turned out, the best—option. They might know the characteristics of the fiber cement board solution from their own experience, or at least they could evaluate it in good faith, since they were as motivated as any other character in the delivery room to find a good answer. After all, they were the ones who would lose the most if the client/father pulled the plug on payments for the project, given the costs they had already incurred in the project to date. By the process of elimination, the project manager had found their most likely ally. So they scheduled a meeting with the contractor—in private, separate from the other characters in the delivery room—to discuss the possible solution and to test whether the idea looked as good to the contractor as it did to them.

The project manager was skilled enough in team dynamics to understand the importance of asking questions about the potential value of their solution instead of arguing that it was best. They introduced their discovery of the fiber cement board option and presented the specifications and as-built examples the supplier had provided. And they asked the contractor a series of questions to give them the opportunity to assess for themselves whether this really was a good answer. Would the material perform as well as the supplier said it would? Could the less extensive excavations be completed in the existing spaces between the villas, preventing the need to destroy any completed buildings to construct the new walls? Could the contractor find a way to bring in the equipment needed to complete these excavations, and was there enough space without demolition to do it? Would the costs of these walls and the excavations stay within the project budget? Did the contractor agree that there was adequate supply of the fiber cement boards to meet the project's demands? Were there any other issues—safety, government regulations, anything the contractor could see from their experience?

It was a complicated discussion; there was a lot to review in a relatively short time. But it was a refreshing change from the shouting matches in the delivery room, and as it turned out, the contractor was intrigued and agreed to get back to them after evaluating the solution in more detail. And the contractor said something else to the project manager that was particularly encouraging: they promised to get back to them as quickly as possible, because they knew time was of the essence, and this might be the last chance to rally the delivery room team around anything that could save the project.

Success, Step Two: Rebuilding the Delivery Room Team to Build a Better Wall

Three days after their initial meeting to discuss the fiber cement board wall solution, the contractor called the project manager with the news that yes, they agreed this was a solution to the issue. Finally, there was not only a potential answer, but also an ally to help advocate for it. But with a delivery room team meeting only three days away, could these two allies convince the other team members? The project manager knew the planning consultant had asked that the agenda include evaluation of one very bad idea the group had discussed when the crisis had first arisen: could construction of the originally-specified walls proceed with a minimum number of villas being destroyed to make room for the excavation equipment? And the project manager also knew the client/father was evaluating a team of day laborers whose leader said they could dig the required excavations by hand (another bad idea). Both ideas had been proposed and rejected by the team weeks earlier, and the project manager saw them for what they were: ammunition for the lawyers that would descend on the delivery room team like vultures after the project/baby had died, so each of these other team members could argue that they had offered a good-faith solution to the issue and perhaps avoid their share of the blame.

The contractor was dismayed to hear what team members were proposing for the next meeting agenda, but the project manager knew a good solution would be welcomed. After all, the development had been highly publicized in trade journals, and many of the villas had been presold to influential community leaders, and—more importantly—to foreign nationals with ties to multinational corporations whose company headquarters had been designed by the planning consultant. If the fiber cement walls met the criteria for a viable replacement and the project/baby could be saved, the project manager knew the meeting would go well. So the two allies went to work preparing a presentation for their solution, and it was added to the agenda for the next team meeting.

Three days later the team gathered, and the contractor couldn't help noticing how quiet the other team members were. When they asked the project manager why this was happening, the project manager provided what should have been an obvious answer: they had contacted the client/father and planning consultant in advance to preview the new solution. And they talked with the other team members about the consequences of failure, not just for the project/baby itself, but also for each of the delivery room team members' future reputations. The previously-scheduled planning discussions about selecting which villas to be demolished, or the hiring of day laborers and training them in how to use jackhammers, were tabled. The project manager had the floor and began a presentation about the fiber cement board solution, delivered in collaboration with the contractor. After many tumultuous meetings since the issue with the boundary walls was first announced, the meeting was anticlimactic. Everyone listened; they asked good questions about cost, schedule, and whether the new walls would stand up as well as the original design—and then they agreed to implement the solution the project manager had discovered. The project/baby was saved and came into the world on time and significantly under budget. A few months after construction was completed, the development was 100 percent sold to the influential residents it was designed to accommodate, and—outside of the team members involved in a dramatic but short-lived blame game—no one was the wiser.

Never underestimate the power of an individual team member dedicated to the health of a project/baby, even when it seems that all is lost and all the other team members have lost their focus. Pray that you never find yourself in the same situation in any of your projects, but if you do, remember that the only way out of a crisis like this is to find a solution that protects the health of the project/baby. And pray that you'll be able to keep your wits about you and be part of that solution.

Lessons Learned: The Power of Self-Fulfilling Prophecies

It's probably clear to readers familiar with projects like this development and its ill-timed boundary walls that an issue this serious is—thankfully—rare. Yet the existence of "gray areas" between the clear responsibilities of delivery room team members is extremely common, should the planning consultant have specified completing all excavations prior to construction of all the project's buildings and walls? Or is that something properly left to the contractor? Should the project manager have scheduled a hypothetical "walk through" of the construction schedule to allow these gray areas to develop before actual construction work began? Should the client/father have written tighter contracts with all members of the delivery room team to require closer collaboration and information-sharing in advance?

Hindsight is always 20/20, so we can be sure that all of the characters in our boundary wall delivery room will adjust their behaviors and procedures in future projects based on their experiences in this unique crisis. But in fact, without the opportunity given them by the project manager to forget the blame game and move on to collaboration on a real solution, the members of this particular delivery room team might just as well have learned from the consequences of a failed project and subsequent lawsuits and financial damages. They could have learned to be more reliant on lawyers and less focused on the talents and skills they need to bring to future delivery room/project teams. Every team member in this example benefited from the singular focus of one individual—the project manager. That is the lesson this example teaches us, and there are two main aspects to this lesson.

The first lesson is *focus on the project*. That's it. When a crisis appears, don't run for the hills and try to protect yourself against a looming failure. If you prepare for a failure, you've already admitted that you're going to fail. And the consequences of failure—except for the learning experiences all human beings gain from our failures—can be catastrophic. Not only can the project/baby itself fail, but one or more members of the delivery room team responsible for the project may face financial losses or damage to their professional reputation that are fatal to them as well. When failure looms, try to do anything possible to avoid it. Save the project/baby at all costs.

The second lesson is that, all other things being equal, *trust the project manager*. In this case—and in fact in many cases—the project manager is the one team member most likely to be aware of the details of any situation; after all, managing the project is the definition of their job. When an issue arises with a construction project/baby, it is most often the project manager who will know about it first. In that respect, our boundary wall example is a common situation: the project manager was the one who first discovered the painful details: to construct the walls as specified, the heavy equipment needed for excavations couldn't be maneuvered into the small spaces between the already-constructed villas. And the project manager would also know the severity of any new issues; whether they were minor and could be addressed in time, or as in this case, they were critical and couldn't be ignored.

In a sense, the behavior of the other team members wasn't all that unusual self-protection is a priority for all human beings, so seeing team members deflect blame or demand a solution from someone else shouldn't have surprised the project manager. And, to be honest, it wouldn't take much self-awareness to help the other team members understand everyone's behavior including their own. But ultimately, the project manager is the character other team members expect will be keeping track everything, discover issues, solve them, or bring important issues to the attention of the team as they are solved.

When issues are minor, the project manager might choose to go directly to the other delivery room character most concerned with an issue, rather than bringing an issue to the attention of everyone. For example, if there were a cost overrun, the project manager could have investigated the reasons behind the cost, and if they were justifiable, could go directly to the client/father for additional funds. Or, if the project faced a scheduling issue, the project manager could contact the contractor to ask to accelerate the work. Perhaps there might be a difference between the overall look and feel of the project in its as-built drawings and the project as it has been constructed. In these cases, the project manager would be the character most likely to discover an issue, to determine how that issue could be solved, and to plan an agenda for the team that is most likely to succeed.

Of course, in our boundary wall example, the issue was not minor. And while the project manager is the one member of the delivery room team responsible for the health of the project/baby, that health is the responsibility of every team member. In times of conflict, when members of the team forget what is important, it is up to the project manager to bring them back to reality: they are all in the delivery room to ensure the completion/delivery of a healthy project/baby.

The good news is that in our boundary wall example, the project manager found a solution that saved the project/baby. The better news is that in most cases, collaboration among two or more delivery room team members is more likely to happen than was the case in this example. In times of crisis, human beings sometimes resort to self-preservation and emotional conflict rather than the rational assessment of an issue and a reasoned search for solutions. In the functioning of a team, such as the construction project/delivery room analogy central to this book, the loss of any single team member to either self-preservation or emotional conflict represents the loss of a potential problem-solver to dysfunctional behavior. When an issue arises, two or three heads trying to solve it are always better than one. But sometimes, one head is all you have. When that head is yours, remember to do your best.

Chapter Three
Learning from Amsterdam and Airliners

Vacuum sewer system

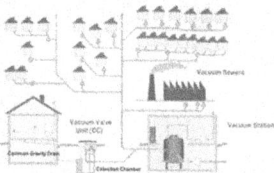

Main characteristics and specifications
- Ideal for demanding ground conditions
- Fast wastewater transport
- Pipes are laid at low depths (80 to 120 cm.)
- Extracted air from the vacuum can be purified

Qua-Vac Vacuflow Sewerage Technology
- Pioneering technology
- Low energy usage
- Robust and reliable
- Low maintainance costs
- Ease of use
- Easy construction

Benefits of the System
- Low water consumption
- Low cost and fast construction times
- No leakage or smell
- Single centralized vacuum station

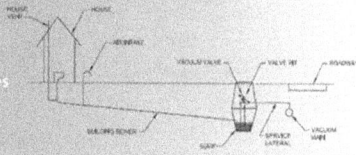

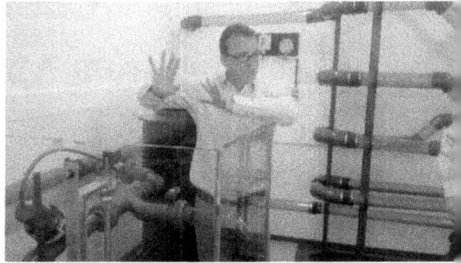

Illustrations:
Last Page: *Supplier schematics of single-pump vacuum sewerage system*
This Page: *Top left, Qua-Vac Team;* ***Top right:*** *demonstration of vacuum flow system;* ***Bottom left:*** *mechanical bowl, including valve control float;* ***Bottom right:*** *single pump and backup at the end of the system.*

Chapter Three
Learning from Amsterdam and Airliners

In this example, the characters in the construction project "Delivery Room" find themselves in a crisis in the middle of building a large development involving more than one hundred thousand square meters of land, with residential buildings and the associated service facilities, including recreation centers, retail space, and central service structures bringing in and distributing electricity, water, sewage, and other infrastructure. In total, there were fifty residential villas and fifteen associated service buildings. Like all the real-life examples in this book, the project had been designed several years prior to construction by architectural consultants, approved by the owner, and a contractor selected to execute the project. As is the case in most projects, each of these characters—the architectural consultant as the "doctor," the owner as the "father," the contractor as the "mother," and the project manager as the "nurse"—played a familiar role, concentrating on matters within their area of expertise and worrying less about matters they considered to be the primary concern of the other characters.

For example, the contractor would behave as most contractors do—enthusiastically planning how to construct the project's buildings first, worrying about infrastructure later. The architectural consultant would similarly focus on the buildings, although from a different point of view. The "doctor" would be more concerned about the look and feel, durability, and performance of the materials used and the creation of a new community that would be functional, attractive, and (at least theoretically) financially successful for the owner. The "father," on the other hand, would be most concerned with keeping construction costs under control, meeting the overall project schedule, and developing a project that would be "sales ready" as soon as possible in order to begin earning income from sales of residential units and the leasing of community buildings and retail facilities.

Most importantly, the project manager would be the one character with an eye toward the overall health of the project in terms of its balance of cost, schedule performance, achievement of the architect/doctor's technical specifications, and the "choreography" of the construction of the project's buildings and infrastructure. The project manager would be selected for their ability to identify issues as early as possible, and solve them as quickly as possible without incurring significantly higher costs or encountering serious delays in meeting the target completion date. The project manager's skills and creativity help the project's other characters—the other people in the delivery room—meet their financial, schedule, and quality objectives, and indeed if the project manager fails to anticipate and solve issues, all of them will suffer their own negative consequences. A contractor who misses schedule milestones or the overall project deadline may face financial penalties imposed by the owner; the consultant responsible for design flaws requiring change orders, or even the failure of building materials or specified systems much later in time may face lawsuits and related financial penalties. The owner, of course, faces the ultimate penalty of all; even if they can shift some of the liability for project failures of any kind to the other characters, it is the owner who will risk financial disaster and even possible bankruptcy if the project doesn't earn the projected income at all, or even in time to cover accrued construction and other development costs before being required to repay the banks and other financial institutions lending money for the project.

Everyone has a stake, in other words, but no one has as much ability to see the project as a whole like the project manager. And when an issue arises, the project manager not only has the advantage of seeing it first, but also has the serious responsibility of finding a solution. In a collaborative effort like the construction of a new residential development—or the successful delivery of a baby once the mother comes to the hospital to give birth—the project manager (or nurse) must find a solution for every issue that arises, and then convince other members of the team to accept that solution to save the project from the risks of leaving the issue unsolved. Creating consensus—the last step in solving an issue on a construction site or in the delivery room—is perhaps the most difficult aspect of this problem-solving process. In this example, creating consensus involves identifying which of the other characters has the most serious risk of harm if the issue is left unsolved, to enlist this character in agreeing on a solution that will work, and to further enlist this character in helping convince the other characters to support and implement the project manager's solution. As a matter of fact, except in the rare case when no other character is willing to sign on to a possible solution—as was the case in the boundary wall example—the most creative and challenging part of a project manager's issue-solving is finding the right partner—in this case the contractor—to begin moving toward a solution and then building an ever larger team willing and able to implement the solution.

The Issue: Maintaining a "Gravity" Sewage System Over Great Distances

When it comes to infrastructure systems, simpler is always better. A sewage system that is constructed in a way that allows for gravity to maintain the flow of liquids through pipes is preferable to the use of pumps to maintain this flow. Mechanical pumps require maintenance, and if they are submerged beneath a building or open land, excavations to get to a faulty piece of mechanical equipment can be costly and disruptive to the residents of a development when repairs are needed. On a more basic level, these mechanical systems require power to operate, meaning there will be a built-in permanent cost of operations that will need to be covered by some form of income—either higher property prices, significant condominium fees, or even rent. It's far simpler to design a system that doesn't require power for ongoing operation, and that also has the lowest possible risk of damage from normal wear and tear.

Theoretically, sewage systems function well using gravity when they maintain a consistent downward slope of 1 percent. Given the fact that a typical building foundation is six meters, or two stories, underground, this 1 percent downward slope requires a lot of excavation even over relatively short distances. For every one hundred meters the system's pipes run, the depth of these pipes and the associated excavation costs will need to account for another meter of depth: seven meters deep after the first one hundred meters, eight meters deep for the next one hundred meters, etc. A large development can quickly involve significant excavation—increasing the initial construction costs and compounding the potential costs for repairs when pipes break or (if they are used) pumps fail.

The project in this case was not only extremely large, but it was being constructed on rocky ground, making excavations for construction and eventual repairs more costly and time-consuming than normal. With the owner, contractor, and consultant each living in their own narrow worlds of responsibilities, it was up to the project manager to foresee the potential issues associated with the development's sewage system. The consultant specified a "sewage system," unaware of the type of soil where the development would be built, and not responsible for selection of the sewage system itself. The contractor might be responsible for selecting and then constructing a sewage system that would work, but was more interested in the buildings than the project's infrastructure, since it is more critical for on-time and within-budget performance to recruit and manage a construction team that can handle the demands of building construction instead of the seemingly "simpler" digging and laying of pipes. For the owner, no news is good news, and if issues are minor enough to stay within specified allowances of 20 percent of the total project estimate, they have little interest in specifics.

But when the rocky condition of the land and the great distances in this development created a need for either significant (and expensive) excavations for a gravity-fed sewage system or a more expensive and risky pump-driven system requiring less digging, it was the project manager who saw the potential for cost overruns in excavation or equipment purchases, and the possible risk to completing the project on schedule. There was a real issue requiring a real solution. But, as is the case with the project manager (or nurse) in most cases, the solution isn't as simple as announcing the issue to the group and trusting them to agree on a reasonable solution. No. What would almost certainly happen in this case would be a rapid argument over who is responsible for the issue, and an effort on each character's part to avoid any potential penalty if they were found to be responsible, or—in the case of the contractor—the opportunity to negotiate for a change order and higher construction fees to cover any additional expenses. Let's see how the project manager found the solution, made sure it would work, and then developed a successful strategy for engaging the team in supporting the solution by picking the right character first.

The Solution: Stretching Gravity with Negative Pressure and Mechanical Bowls

The project manager found a solution that had been used since the 1970s in similar construction projects—even longer when they considered systems used to drain excess water from the lowlands of Amsterdam, or to flush the toilets on modern airliners. It was negative pressure; a single pump at the end of the sewage system would be used to draw fluids from the entire length of the system's pipes. Negative pressure would assist in draining of fluids through the system's pipes, in much the same way that opening the pipe in an airliner's toilet draws fluid out of this very small system.

But a large development with more than sixty buildings (or, for that matter, an entire city like Amsterdam) would require an enormous pump to keep liquids flowing through the system without using gravity. But to use gravity would mean dealing with the ever-deeper excavation of a 1 percent slope over thousands of meters. The solution the project manager found was a system that eliminated the need for sloped pipes altogether through the use of a series of shorter, level pipes linked together with "mechanical bowls" every six villas or so that would hold fluids temporarily. These bowls are equipped with a float inside them, much like what can be found in every toilet tank, allowing these fluids to rise in the bowl until the liquid level is high enough to pull open a closed valve connecting the bowl to the next pipe on the way to a final pumping station at the end of the line. This single pump maintains constant negative pressure on the system, although it works only when each mechanical bowl is full enough to raise the float and open its valve. When this happens, fluid from the

37

full bowl is drawn into the pipe leading to the next bowl, until it drains enough to lower the float and shut the valve. Similarly, that next mechanical bowl functions exactly like the first one, filling with fluids until its float is lifted, opening a valve to its drainage pipe leading to the next bowl down the line. As waste water drains from one mechanical bowl into the next pipe, the process repeats as necessary until all waste is drained into the final bowl located in the system's pumping station, where it can be removed from the system and transported away.

Because the entire system maintains negative pressure provided by the vacuum pump at the end, whenever these valves open, this pressure draws fluid through the pipes; there is only one way for the liquid to flow. The central pump is located in the basement level of a building, so if it needs servicing, no excavation is required (a second backup pump is also located in this facility, ready to kick in should anything happen to the primary pump). The system's mechanical bowls are simple devices with no power requirements of their own— only floats. They are inexpensive and, since they allow the entire system to function without gravity, they are never deep enough to require significant excavation for any possible repairs. In fact, they can be constructed as chambers that are accessible via manhole covers for easy access.

The system is based on sound science—it does not need the standard 1 percent slope required for sewage systems; the mechanical bowls operate in the same fashion as common toilet tanks; and the overall power requirements to maintain negative pressure are constant due to the linearity of the pipes between the mechanical bowls. Even better, it was not only sound in theory—the system could be observed in practice by going to Amsterdam and seeing it in action.

Moreover, the system had the added advantage of being inexpensive in terms of equipment required—no powered pumps except at the end, and simple mechanical bowls accessible via manhole covers every six villas or so. Eliminating the need for any sloping of the pipes between villas also kept excavation costs low. The negative pressure of the entire system was not only sound for maintaining a working sewage system over time, it also had the added benefit of containing the effects of any possible leaks caused by broken pipes. Typically, a pipe full of fluid leaks out when it breaks, causing a need for cleanup in addition to repair of the pipe itself. But with negative pressure, a broken pipe would suck surrounding dirt into the pipe—the fluid would not leak out. In fact, while repairs would certainly be required to repair any breaks, this negative pressure would give maintenance and management staff time to effect repairs for a time before surrounding earth would block the pipe, and the location of mechanical bowls every six villas in length would also help pinpoint the location of any break.

With the single pump able to purify air extracted from the system, there was also ample opportunity to minimize any odor in addition to the minimal risk of leaks. The system was inexpensive to build, reliable and inexpensive to operate, and environmentally friendly. In short, it was a perfect solution. Now, having found such a solution, the project manager was faced with the next step in problem solving: finding the all-important first ally among project team members to bring the solution into practice.

Selecting a Partner: Identifying the System's Primary Benefit— and Beneficiary

The project manager would now be faced with the challenge of bringing the rest of the team to consensus so they could work together in constructing a sewage system that would keep the project on schedule and within budget, with the added benefit of being able to operate reliably with minimal maintenance over time and even function in a way that would be more environmentally friendly than a number of more expensive and risky alternatives. The project manager (or, as we know them from our delivery room analogy, the "nurse") knew it was likely that everyone would agree on the solution if it were presented correctly, but they also knew that if the wrong character was recruited to help with the initial "sale" to the rest of the team, it might be the case that the self-interest of a poorly-chosen partner could result in failure.

How? Well, for example, if the architectural consultant were enlisted first, they might not want to be seen as having failed to pay attention to this important aspect of the program, or risk attack by other team members eager to place blame on anyone but themselves. They might be more likely to tell the project manager that they had no responsibility for solving the issue, since it was never their responsibility to design or specify a working sewage system in the first place. And there might be enough "gray area" in the design documents to allow an argument like this to continue for quite some time, jeopardizing the project schedule on its own. Similarly, the contractor might not want to agree to sell the solution to the rest of the team because it could be in their best financial interest to claim that it was a design flaw, qualifying for a change order and an increase in construction fees to "design" a new system and then build it. A similar time-consuming argument could ensue with the same consequences as one begun by a self-interested consultant.

That leaves the owner (the "father" in our delivery room analogy), who of course turned out to be the right choice as ally number one for the project manager. With the primary benefits being cost savings and adherence to the original project schedule, the owner would be the logical choice in this case. But in some ways, since all issues that occur in the middle of a construction project almost always threaten the project budget and schedule, this could lead an inexperienced project manager to always go to the owner first whenever an issue arises. In fact, it is normally not a good idea, since an owner who is not familiar with the realities of construction details would most likely go to the team member they trust the most. After all, they hired the team in the first place, and probably have a preconceived idea of each member's skills. An owner who trusts the architect (the "doctor" in the delivery room) would simply take the project manager's idea to that team member and bring the process of agreeing on a solution to the same stage as if the project manager went to the architect first. Or, if the owner trusts the contractor (the "mother"), that team member would have the advantage of having implied support for a change order from an owner seeking their guidance in solving the issue.

The reason going to the owner as the first ally in solving this issue was that this owner/developer was a large corporation, with experience in similar developments and a staff that included people familiar with the details of not only marketing buildings to consumers, but also the actual process of constructing the development in the first place. The project manager knew the owner's internal staff would understand the sophisticated details of the negative pressure/mechanical bowl system, and that they would most likely use this understanding to agree to the merits of the solution.

Based on this assessment of the team's skills, capabilities, and motivations, the project manager went to the owner to present the solution and invited the owner's representatives to go with them to Amsterdam to see that city's water table management system in practice. Of course, the invitation process required a number of technical presentations, supported by the company that manufactures the system. Because the cost savings were so impressive—both during construction and ongoing operations—the client's staff could make its own informed decision to go with the project manager's recommendations. By going to these staff members before approaching the client's senior management, the project manager was also able to enlist their enthusiastic support because now they were in a position to tell their bosses that they had found a solution that would work, that would keep the project on schedule, and that would save money. The project manager didn't need to take credit for the solution as much as they needed to make sure the right solution was selected and implemented.

What happened next was that the client's senior management, having been convinced by their staff and the project manager of the benefits of the solution, went to the architect and sold the solution to *them*. And the client decided to fund the inspection team, involving their own staff, the architect, and the project manager. The contractor didn't go, but instead agreed that if the solution satisfied these other team members, they would work directly with the supplier of the sewage system in constructing the project's infrastructure. And so three of the four project team's key members went to Amsterdam, observed an entire city successfully using the proposed gravity/mechanical bowl system, and agreed to adopt it for their project. They returned to tell the contractor to get in touch with the supplier, who agreed (how could they not?), and the project continued without any further issues—at least not with respect to the sewage system.

Lessons Learned: It's Always Something

The problem-solving skills required of a project manager in charge of the construction of a large development always require the related skills of keen observation, anticipation of potential consequences, diligent research, creative thinking, and excellent people skills. This is why issues that threaten budgets and schedules, or quality and performance, are often identified by the project manager before they become obvious to others. Whether it's a sewage system not fully considered before construction, the need to change specified materials based on concerns that become apparent during construction, or the realization that a project's budget or schedule is in jeopardy, the project manager is generally the one to see these things first. It's not just because of the project manager's skills—even though the best of these skilled professionals have all of the qualities identified earlier in this paragraph—it's because solving issues is the project manager's *job*.

Issues arise on construction projects for a few predictable reasons. First, there is always a great deal of activity on the site. And most of the people are deeply involved in their own specialized part of the project—excavating foundations or trenches for pipes and electrical systems; framing buildings to allow for efficient construction of floors, walls, and building systems later; or installing the electrical, water, or HVAC systems when the project has reached the time for these activities. None of these specialists is looking at the big picture. They're already working on the site; they're under some pressure to get their work done within specified quality, budget, and schedule parameters, and that's usually enough for them to worry about. If they do their job as expected and follow the requirements of the project's design documents and construction methods, there is no need to look for any better solution. Until there is an urgent issue, of course. And when there is, it's time to contact the project manager.

Sometimes, it's the realization that a high-voltage cable has been laid and a building that is supposed to be constructed above it can't be built there without relocating the cable or moving the building. It's usually the combination of two or more small details like these that create a big issue. In the case of this sewage example, it was a realization by the contractor that the need to excavate increasingly deep trenches for gravity-fed sewage lines through rocky soil would create schedule and budget issues during construction. That initial issue was compounded by the project manager's realization that these deep pipes would be hard to maintain in the event of any breaks or leaks, increasing the risks the owner would face for many years. It was up to the project manager to evaluate the initial issue discovered by the contractor, and extrapolate the possible consequences of this issue even if it were successfully overcome during construction.

The time between the initiation of a project and the beginning of construction is usually long—it can take a year or more to finish design documents, and several months more to price the approved design before it's put out to contractors for bid. During this time, there is plenty of opportunity for issues to be made, and these issues aren't necessarily caught through any theoretical review of design documents. Most of them are discovered when a project is underway. And when these issues are discovered, the initial decision-makers are often out of the picture. It's up to people on the ground to solve these issues; the only advantage in involving absent initial decision-makers is to assign serious financial liability in the event an issue becomes a project-threatening problem.

The good news is that many of them are minor issues, absorbed by contingency allowances in every project budget and schedule. But sometimes, they are large and require a serious reconsideration of the way the project will be constructed, the materials that will be used, and—if things are serious enough or not managed properly—they jeopardize the overall financial success of the project, and possibly the financial health of one or more of the team members.

Experienced project managers know there are zero cases of all major issues being solved before they become a crisis during the construction process. It's part of the game. The implementers who are present when these issues develop are not the initial decision-makers. They're often not even senior people in the contractor, design consultant, or owner's organizations. They're employees and, often, they're not technically skilled. They always have a boss or a board of directors they need to consider as much as they are interested in the actual solution to a real issue. And they have excuses. "But we already designed that," or, "We hired the best design consultants." The successful project manager needs to get their attention and find a way to build momentum for agreeing on real solutions to real issues instead of looking for excuses.

That's where the people skills come in. Who is most likely to be at greatest risk if the issue goes unsolved? Who is most respected by other group members? Who has the technical knowledge to understand the benefits of a proposed solution? Who is more likely to fight for their self-interest instead of agreeing to implement a good solution? Whose arm needs to be twisted, and when?

These skills may come into play late in the process of solving an issue on a construction site—long after the issue becomes apparent, long after its possible impact on the project's/baby's health is found to be serious, and long after a possible solution has been found and even tested. But these people skills are always among the most important qualifications for a good project manager. In the case of this development's sewage system, selecting the owner as the first ally in agreeing on a solution was as vital as the technical quality of the solution itself.

Chapter Four

When the Project Must Be Completed on Time, No Matter What

Light Weight Steel Structure and Fiber Cement Board

HEKIMBOARD Fiber Cement Board

- Eco-friendly — (Protects the environment)
- Contains no toxic materials — (Contains no asbestos)
- Resistent to extreme weather conditions — (Heat and water resistant)

Benefits of the System
- Resistant
- Cost effective
- Quick instalation

Galvanized steel structure
- High-end technology design
- Easy instalation

Illustration: Lightweight fiber cement board and galvanized steel prefabricated structural systems not only improve project value metrics, they also allow for environmental and aesthetic achievements in many cases.

Chapter Four
When the Project Must Be Completed on Time, No Matter What

In this example, the characters in the construction project "Delivery Room" were engaged in an enormous residential project involving more than five hundred buildings. There were basically five styles of villas, each applied to about one hundred structures. The wrinkle in this project was the fact that it had a "hard" completion date deadline. The people who would live in this development would be employed in a major energy exploration project. They needed to be on site when the project began, in much the same way that Olympic athletes need to be living in a city's Olympic Village on the first day of the Games. Delay was not an option. The owner stood to profit greatly if the project was completed on time, but the penalties for being even a little late would mean financial ruin.

Of course, as fate would have it, the project was begun and well underway when it became apparent that there was a serious risk that construction would be late. Like other projects of this scale, there was significant time between completion of architectural design documents and the beginning of work by the contractor. This was itself not beyond the initial project schedule—no one was technically late when the contractor began work. What had changed, however, was that the local economy had significantly improved since the project was originally planned, and thus the labor market was tight. The contractor was having difficulty finding the number of workers needed to build five hundred buildings within the specified schedule. And, given the nature of the materials specified in the original design documents, there was no alternative to complete the structures more quickly without changing design specifications.

Specifically, those specifications called for "traditional" construction methods, beginning with digging of a foundation, then construction of columns, and building walls with poured concrete. There were no issues with the site itself, or with the availability of construction materials and on-time delivery. The issue was strictly a shortage of labor, combined with the fact that, based on the architect's design and specified materials, it would essentially take the same time to build each villa regardless of how many there were. Each building would take five months to complete.

That would be true if there were one villa or five hundred. But there was no way for the contractor to hire and manage enough workers to build five hundred of them at once. He might be able to find enough specialized steel workers, concrete workers, and building finishers to build one hundred villas at a time, but the total project schedule would therefore be five times the five months each one hundred villas would require. And this twenty-five-month schedule would mean the entire project would be late. Unless something changed, there would be no healthy building/baby.

The alternative solution was not a complicated one: the project manager and all other team members knew that relying on prefabricated structures built in a factory and assembled on site was the way to solve concerns about the project's schedule. While the foundations would still need to be built for each of the five hundred buildings, the lightweight steel and fiber cement board structural elements could be built to suit any design; modern factories can meet this challenge; they are 100 percent flexible in their ability to produce all the elements required for each of the five villa designs.

The issue was in creating consensus around this solution, specifically with one team member: ironically, the contractor. On the face of it, with the difficulty in hiring enough workers to stay on schedule, one would think the contractor would welcome the prefabricated solution. But in fact, the contractor resisted any change to a solution involving prefabricated building elements. Their reasons were mostly based on avoiding any sort of risk. They were unfamiliar with prefabricated buildings, and preferred to stay with the familiar processes of the original design. To be fair, they had bid on the project based on their confidence in being able to complete the project on time using traditional poured-concrete methods. They were also worried whether there would be enough prefabricated building elements available to meet the needs for constructing five hundred buildings within the schedule. The factory that could produce these prefabricated elements was in Turkey, and the contractor was concerned about the distance required for shipping, the ability to communicate design specifications to a foreign company, and the risk of relying on a single factory to produce all the required building materials.

These were all legitimate concerns, but in fact the contractor was using these objections to mask their real mindset, which was: even if the project were late, it wouldn't be their problem. They believed they were being asked to assume new risks by working with unfamiliar materials from a single factory in a foreign country, instead of working as best they could within the parameters of the project as they had described in their winning bid. The other characters in the construction project/delivery room were willing to consider the prefabricated materials option, but they could not complete the project without the contractor going along. They needed more than agreement; they knew the contractor could always claim any missed deadline was not their responsibility and were concerned that the contractor might simply not try hard enough to meet the schedule if they forced this new option onto the project. It was an interesting challenge for the project manager; instead of trying to find a single "first ally," in this case, they had to overcome a single "unwilling ally." And because of the serious financial damages the other characters would suffer if the project was late, they were unwilling to pressure the contractor instead of looking for a way to bring them along as enthusiastic partners in implementing a new solution.

The complication of potential liability was primary factor in the issue the project manager had to solve in this case. The architectural consultant was worried about the performance of the prefabricated buildings over time, and thought that use of these new materials would affect their liability about the "means and methods" used in executing their design. The reinforced concrete specified in their original design had been approved by the owner, specifically around these materials' durability and load capacity. If the owner agreed to a new design, then the design consultant's durability and load liability could be renegotiated. But if the consultant did not agree to the new materials and they were in fact used, then the contractor would assume the liability for the new materials' durability and load. It was easy to see why no one wanted to make the first move. And yet everyone could see that, without any change, the project would be late and serious penalties were likely.

A Creative Solution: May the Best Methods and Materials Win

The project manager's solution in this case was a brilliant way to engage the contractor in deciding whether the proposed new construction materials and methods would in fact be better than the original design. The project manager proposed a test of both the original design using poured reinforced concrete and the new prefabricated lightweight steel and fiber cement board option. The contractor would build two identical villas (mock-ups), one using each method. Following completion of this test, the entire team would evaluate which one was better and use this information to decide how to proceed with the entire development. If the new prefabricated option were selected, it would be a change of scope for the contractor, who would not be held liable for the "methods and materials" liability they feared.

The test began with the contractor convinced the original reinforced concrete method would be superior, but in fact their workers finished the new mock-up early enough that they never finished the traditional mock-up. Both the client and consultant approved of the change, and the project proceeded with the prefabricated option. But that wasn't the end of the story. There were still challenges to meet in implementing the new construction methodology and in ensuring that all team members were comfortable with the liability implications of the change. Still, as we will see below, these were details to be managed in ways that are familiar to anyone involved who has many changes in a large project.

The revolutionary accomplishment of the project manager in this case was the realization that no one would step up voluntarily to adopt a new system—*even with almost certain schedule failure staring them in the face*—so it was necessary to create consensus in a way that would allow everyone to make their own judgment on the relative merits of the two possible ways forward. Taking time out of an already-threatened project schedule to conduct a mock-up test of these two methods was an enormous risk; however, it was a manageable risk as far as the schedule was concerned, as it could overlap with other activities for site preparation. The benefit of the mock-up was that it eliminated the more serious risks that the project would continue to move forward with a doomed construction scheme, or that it would be delayed for an indefinite period while the parties negotiated about shifting liability before resuming construction at all. Sometimes you must walk the tightrope without a net.

The Details of the Solution: Performance Is Everything. So Is Consensus.

In reality, the contractor in this example was in deep trouble, and it's hard to understand their resistance to the prefabricated solution at first glance. Think about it. They couldn't get enough skilled workers to complete the project using familiar methods, yet they held fast to those familiar methods until they reluctantly discovered the benefits of the new prefabricated solution. Why would they do this? As we discussed earlier, they were certainly motivated by the possible assumption of new liability risk. If they agreed to follow the client and abandon the design consultant's original design, they would have assumed enormous new risks. What if the prefabricated materials weren't as durable or strong as advertised? What if they were delayed en route from Turkey, or if the factory couldn't meet the demands to manufacture all the required prefabricated elements? Without renegotiating their new liabilities, these risks would all become the responsibility of the contractor.

But there was also something else happening behind the scenes. The contractor was one of several contractors in their city, and had won the bid by defeating all their competitors. But the project in this case was so large that many subcontractors would be needed to provide the labor required to construct five hundred buildings on such an aggressive schedule. Who were these subcontractors? None other than the unsuccessful bidders. Throughout the project, regardless of what methods and materials were selected, the contractor would face the constant risk that these competitors/subcontractors might not meet their commitments, either out of jealousy, or because in the booming local economy, they could make more money by abandoning the contractor to work on their own new projects. These risks were real for the contractor, yet the contractor would never reveal them to the consultant or client. But because the project manager knew the local construction industry, they knew about these risks and understood what they meant for the contractor—good and bad. The project manager could sympathize with the contractor when subcontractors might abandon the project for more lucrative work. But the project manager also knew that the contractor could invent design flaws or other false reasons for construction delays that were really caused by labor shortages.

Knowing the way the local industry operated in times of stress was a valuable asset for the project manager in this case. They knew that with labor shortages being the critical path that needed to be navigated, a solution reducing the need for on-site labor—in this case, buying prefabricated elements from factories in Turkey—was the best option. Then, with this optimal solution clearly in mind, it was time for the project manager to find a way to gain consensus around it, even when gaining that consensus meant risking valuable time to allow the contractor to feel like they were part of the solution instead of having it forced upon them. And ultimately, every one of the characters in the construction project/delivery room needed to approve the new solution. Otherwise, there could be no agreement on where liability would lie once this new construction method began. As it turned out, once the design consultant agreed on the new construction method, there was no shift in liability from the original agreement, and the contractor was protected in the same way as they would have been the case if no change in methodology were adopted.

Minor Tweaks: Project Management Never Sleeps

In a project as enormous as this, with so many buildings needing to be completed so the client/father could be paid, and the enormous risk of being penalized instead if construction were late, solving this one issue wasn't the only challenge for our project manager. Some of these follow-up challenges involved being flexible; others meant continued adjustments in construction methods, even after everyone agreed to move forward with prefabricated steel and fiber cement board.

For one thing, the contractor had committed to using a labor force that would be composed of 20 percent of their own workers and 80 percent from outside subcontractors. That was never achieved due to the local economy's shortage of available labor. The project manager could have cited the contractor for violating these terms, or at least faulted them for not working hard enough to recruit outside laborers, but they chose to ignore this technical matter and concentrate instead on meeting the project's aggressive completion deadline. By supporting the contractor in meeting these schedule requirements, the team was eventually able to complete a single building with a team of ten workers in twenty-one days.

In order to mitigate the contractor's perceived risk that a single factory might not be capable of manufacturing and delivering all the prefabricated building elements on time, the project manager agreed to source these materials to three separate companies, so that no single company could put the project at risk. And when it came to helping the contractor use their staff to their maximum value, the project manager also agreed to allow some of the development's buildings—particularly the clubhouse, nursery school, facilities buildings, and playgrounds and pools—to be built with traditional poured-concrete methods. This allowed the contractor to have someplace to employ their workers when they couldn't work on the prefabricated buildings, allowing them to absorb these fixed labor costs while moving forward on construction of noncritical path structures. This was also the case in pouring foundations—the one aspect of each of the five hundred villas that couldn't be accelerated using prefabricated materials. Finally, in keeping with the practice of not approving 100 percent prefabricated construction, the project manager decided against purchasing the prefabricated structures' electrical and plumbing systems and interior finishings. In part, this was to meet local construction codes, but it was also because some of the villas were sold as "luxury" residences requiring more high-end interiors.

Lessons Learned

In my continuing study of the challenges that arise during construction projects large and small, and the fact that the project manager is most often the one individual called on to address these challenges and solve issues for the entire team, I want to remind readers that there are always issues in any such project. It's never too late for them to appear; even when all appears to be set and every team member is working diligently on the way to completion, something will happen. It's just the nature of the beast. Experienced project managers know this and understand the importance of keeping one's perspective when another team member comes forward with an issue that must be solved quickly. That perspective is part of a way of thinking all project managers need to adopt in performing their duties. When an issue arises, it's time to keep calm, analyze the situation, think of both the immediate concerns as well as possible longer-term consequences, and then begin to look for a solution.

The combination of professional skills—analysis, anticipation, solid research, and evaluation of alternatives—with people skills—the ability to keep calm, stay confident, and communicate well with colleagues—are what makes for a strong project manager. Big issues in construction projects often bring emotional reactions among team members. Some of them may stand to lose a great deal if things get worse, or if the issue cannot be solved quickly. They will probably be incapable of coming up with solutions on their own, but that won't stop them from demanding a solution from other people, along with threats to make sure someone else "pays" for what they surely define as a "problem" and not an issue. Doing one's best to manage the interpersonal situation among team members is the project manager's responsibility; but as important as it is, it is only a means to an end. Keeping the team calm buys time for the project manager to find a solution, test whether it will actually work, and then begin the final task of building consensus for embarking on a new successful path toward completion. Keeping everyone calm without solving the issue isn't good enough, so my advice is to remember the balance between professional and people skills means focusing on both sides of this delicate equation.

It's helpful for the project manager to think ahead to achieve these two objectives—and to do this when everything is going well. In this chapter's example, it was clear that an overheated local economy would lead to a labor shortage, and that the largest construction projects would feel the effects of this shortage. By being aware of the likelihood that there might not be enough workers to build five hundred villas on time without streamlining the need for labor, the project manager should have thought of possible solutions before the issue became obvious to the contractor and other team members. Knowing that prefabricated building elements would reduce the need for on-site labor by transferring this responsibility to workers in foreign factories made it possible to stay on schedule in the face of local labor shortages. An additional understanding of the contractor's place among other contractors who were once competitors in bidding for the job and then became subcontractors would also help the project manager address the stresses associated with the contractor's search for qualified labor. The project manager could also anticipate that the other contractors might not cooperate as fully as necessary in keeping their commitments to supply labor, making it even more urgent to look for a solution that wouldn't rely on these other companies and their ability to supply vast numbers of construction workers.

A project manager who knows the potential issues faced by other team members, understands how difficult they may be to solve, and the worries that would result for a company like the contractor in this example, forges bonds with colleagues and builds more trust among the team. This trust becomes a valuable asset when the potential solution to a serious issue seems unorthodox, or when questions of potential shifts in liability keep team members from acting voluntarily. Without the trust of fellow team members, the project manager in this example could probably never have convinced the design consultant and client to approve the mock-up of two different construction methods with a hard deadline looming and getting closer every day.

And without that mock-up, I believe there would not have been time to solve the labor shortage issue before the required completion date passed without a finished project. It could have been a disaster for everyone, and no one else could have provided the leadership required to avoid it.

It's also important for a project manager to recognize a good idea. In this case, using prefabricated building components was a standard theoretical approach and, if it worked, this solution would be a good way to reduce the need for a huge number of construction workers. It didn't matter who thought of the idea first; what mattered was that it had an excellent chance of working. In this case, the challenge for the project manager wasn't finding the solution; it was convincing reluctant team members that the solution needed to be adopted even though each of them had valid reasons for resisting it. In other cases, the project manager must be willing to consider good ideas that might be brought to the table by another team members. If the contractor had worked with prefabricated building elements before (they hadn't, of course), they might have brought the idea to the team at the same time they saw how seriously local labor shortages threatened the project schedule. Or maybe the owner had a colleague or even (God forbid) a relative in Turkey who owned a factory capable of manufacturing the prefabricated building elements this project needed. In either case, the project manager would need to put aside any prejudices against these ideas based on their source and focus solely on the quality of these suggested solutions.

Separating preconceived attitudes about potential solutions from an impartial evaluation of them turned out to be an important part of the successful completion of this project. Remember, the design consultant was concerned about liability consequences if the project changed its strategy from pouring reinforced concrete to buying prefabricated lightweight steel and fiber cement board. Further, the contractor didn't want to take on a new construction methodology on a project this large—working in unfamiliar territory was understandably frightening given the consequences of something going wrong that might make the contractor entirely liable for a delay. As I learned firsthand on this project, the contractor was hoping that relying on original construction methods would prove superior to the prefabricated solution during the mock-up project they agreed to undertake. It took more than just confidence in the new solution for the project manager to arrange for the contractor's building of two separate mock-ups. It required a willingness to take on the risk that a team member biased against the better idea would prove the "wrong" solution better. Sometimes a project manager needs to be brave in addition to being right.

In the end, success for the project manager in this example also required doing their homework. Any solution would need to respect the other team members' concern about shifting liability and the possibility that they would be asked to assume more risk in the new arrangement than they agreed to assume at the beginning of the project. This was handled by arranging an impartial test that showed the contractor they could meet the schedule; it also gave the design consultant the opportunity to study the durability, strength, and other qualities of the prefabricated materials. With this study complete, the consultant was able to approve the new solution, and this approval kept everyone's liability arrangements in place. They could move forward with a solution that would keep the project on schedule.

But there was also another aspect of the project that needed consideration. Would the new method also keep the project within budget? The project manager had to be skilled enough to forecast the actual budget impact of this solution before proposing it. That would require careful consideration of all potential costs—design of the prefabricated components prior to their being manufactured overseas, the actual prices of the components in the quantities required for the entire project, shipping charges, labor costs for the reduced construction team that would assemble these parts on site, and other expenses. The idea of keeping some elements of the project apart from the prefabricated solution would also require calculation of the costs of constructing the service buildings with poured concrete, as would the decision to separate building systems such as plumbing and electrical lines from the prefabricated solutions. The project budget is always a collection of moving parts, and I believe the parties in this project would never have approved the new solution without confidence that the budget impact was carefully considered.

The fact that the project manager could anticipate consequences of the proposed solution carefully enough to assure it would meet schedule, budget, and quality requirements made it possible to advocate effectively for a solution that may have been obviously correct, but that also may have been rejected by a team composed of individual members more concerned with their own self-interests than the health of the project/baby overall. A project manager who can "read" the mindset of team members and understand what motivates them can cross that final bridge on the way to success—building consensus for the best solution to an issue. Knowing that they were all concerned about risk and took a conservative approach to management of this extremely large and important project gave the project manager the intellectual guidance needed to keep the proposed solution within the bounds of what they would consider a good plan.

The project manager sold this solution as one that would keep the project on its original schedule, control costs well enough to keep it within the parameters of the original budget, and manage the risks and liability of all team members within those they had agreed to assume at the beginning of the project. And given a skeptical group of colleagues, the project manager's most important contribution to the solution was the series of steps taken to win the confidence of team members in the benefits of replacing poured concrete construction with the use of prefabricated building elements. Arranging for a risky, but ultimately successful, test of the solution on site by the team itself was the capstone of this project manager's success.

Sometimes, in order to assure risk-averse project team members that a proposed solution is the right way to go, the project manager needs to assume a lot of risk on their own.

Chapter Five
Always Test before You Build

Water for landscaping

Main characteristics of QXT-Plant
- It is a composition of natural minerals and organic additives
- Developed for savings in irrigation and more biological activity
- Better retains water in the root of plants and trees
- Contains components necesary for a good quality soil
- QXT-Plant has a "Positive irritating effect" which enhances the formation of new roots

Benefits of the System
- 50% water savings
- 50% more biologic activity of the soil
- Fast decomposition of dead plant cellulose
- 30% more nitrogen in the soil
- 30% more green mass and crop
- Reduced pumping, storage and maintainance cost

Illustration: Application of modern technology to landscaping can yield surprising benefits in terms of conservation and customization of soil characteristics, allowing for increased biodiversity in arid or otherwise difficult environments.

Chapter Five
Always Test Before You Build

In this example, our characters were constructing a beach palace for the royal family of Qatar. They enjoyed nature and the weather, so their private retreat would need to include not only luxurious buildings, but also spectacular landscaping. Plans called for the planting of several beautiful one thousand-year-old trees to be imported from Spain, and it was clear to those who had assessed the site that the sandy soil and intrusion of salty water at high tide created a serious risk of whether these exotic trees—or any landscaping plants—could survive. The risks were already significant in the project management team's mission of constructing a vacation residence for the royal family; no one wanted to provide them with anything less than a completely stunning and beautiful residence. The fact that this challenge went beyond the buildings themselves to creation of an artificial "natural world" only added to the pressure to make sure everything was first-class.

Consistent with my project management philosophy, we began with a small-scale mock-up that could serve as a preview for the royal family before we began to build the entire complex. This included a small two-story building—basically a master bedroom with a bathroom and balcony overlooking a sample of our landscaping, to show them interior furnishings and finishes and the type of view they could expect when they looked outside. We fully intended to demolish this preliminary building and incorporate the bedroom and balcony within one of the larger, permanent buildings.

We had four months to construct the mock-up and associated landscaping, a time that we had already built into the overall project schedule. In addition to the phrases I've introduced in this book so far, such as "there is no such thing as a problem, only issues with solutions," or, "fail to plan = plan to fail," here's another to remember: "mock-ups are a must." I can point to several real-life examples, including the story told in this chapter, where mock-ups have identified tomorrow's issues today, giving our team time to find and implement a solution that we otherwise might not have discovered, tested, and installed.

While the contractor's small team of construction workers built the bedroom and balcony demonstration building, another team of landscapers planted a test garden below the balcony, between the building and the sea. Independently of the landscaping improvements, the mock-up building was raised to avoid the risk of flooding at high tide. At the same time, the landscaping team added additional freshwater irrigation systems. However, within four weeks, all the demonstration plants died. We were unsure what the problem was (I can use the word "problem," because the plants had, in fact, died) and, unfortunately, the landscaping professionals on our team were as baffled as we were. I knew we would need to find a solution quickly enough so we wouldn't jeopardize the overall twenty-four-month project schedule. Even more important, we couldn't risk having any of the royal family's one thousand-year-old trees die on the site.

Our team's landscaping manager identified a possible solution. He knew a local expert who had finished his PhD at Leal University in France, focusing on project management and strategic planning, and applying his methods on agricultural projects. This expert had also conducted successful research work on the irrigation of land deemed otherwise unsuitable for any sort of plantings. We agreed to contact him and explain our situation. The PhD researcher came to our site and, after testing the site's soil and water, told us we had two separate issues to solve: (1) the need for a more robust freshwater irrigation system, and (2) improvements to the soil so it could support our intended plantings.

We were ready for the irrigation recommendation; it seemed likely to us that there was still possible seepage of salty water from the nearby sea, or at least that the soil was already contaminated with salt water from many years of flooding at high tide. But we didn't expect the need to improve the soil itself beyond clearing it of salt water. Our expert explained to us that he had a proven method for improving the quality of our site's soil based on four years of research and testing.

His solution involved the introduction of "good" bacteria to replace the "bad" bacteria that were prevalent on our site. He told us that his tests of our site's soil found that 99 percent of the bacteria were bad and needed to be replaced. He told us about his soil improvement system and how he had created a new strain of bacteria that, once introduced into any soil, would convert it into a fertile environment for all kinds of plants. He said he could introduce his "good" bacteria into the soil on our site, and we could repeat our previously failed test plantings in time to keep our project schedule intact. We agreed that we would inject his good bacteria into the soil between our test balcony and the sea, plant another test garden, and watch to see if it worked.

But the issues with our landscaping wouldn't be completely overcome with this innovative and—to those of us who listened to him—almost unbelievable solution. There was still the matter of irrigation. He told us that before beginning our next test garden, we would likely need more help with our irrigation system than we had originally thought. In the process, he also provided us with a solution that would control costs we thought had been unavoidable in creating a tropical garden on a sandy desert beach. He proposed a solution that would save water.

Our expert explained that with no rain or natural water on site, we were probably going to need sixteen liters of water per square meter per day to grow grasses alone. Without any additional work to design a more efficient water delivery system, a single palm tree would need two hundred liters per day. These costs had been roughly anticipated by our team's landscapers and were included in the project's "water" budget for ongoing operations at the completed palace complex. Since these costs were not in its "plantings" budget, the cost category we were spending in our mock-up phase, we weren't concerned with it now.

So, without the PhD expert's help, we would have simply gone forward with the introduction of his "good" bacteria, and if it worked, continued with our originally designed irrigation system, resigning ourselves to spending the original exorbitant budget on irrigation, which the royal family had already approved and, in fact, could certainly afford. Our expert said he could save the project—and the royal family—a lot of money on irrigation by further improving the soil we were planning to use in our tropical garden.

He explained that the plants cited in his (and our) budget estimates weren't benefitting from all the water that would be delivered every day. Grasses didn't get to absorb all sixteen liters per square meter per day, and neither did the palm trees use all their two hundred liters per day per tree. In reality, much of this water would simply drain away into the soil below the garden; his estimates were that this loss would range from between 25 percent to as much as 75 percent of the water provided each day. And, because he also believed in only introducing issues with an accompanying solution for them, he told us he could help us install a system that would cut our water requirements in half. His solution was to further improve our landscaping soil by introducing volcanic rocks. These would absorb irrigation water and keep it from seeping away. Grasses would only need eight liters per square meter per day, and palm trees would thrive on one hundred liters per day each.

To be honest, while I had gone to visit the PhD expert's research gardens to see with my own eyes how his combination of good bacteria and volcanic soil performed as advertised, the rest of my team thought his proposal too good to be true. And the contractor rightly pointed out that the costs of his soil improvement techniques were beyond the budget for planting soil in his original landscaping budget. But since we had already exhausted ourselves in searching for other solutions to keep our test garden from dying, and because we did have a schedule for the royal family to come and inspect the mock-up building and landscaping in a couple of months, we went ahead with our test, installed the expert's bacteria and volcanic rocks, and watched our next garden not only survive, but thrive.

Luckily for us, our expert was also a good salesman and had anticipated our budget concerns regarding the cost of his bacteria and volcanic-rock soil. He knew that these costs could be recouped over a few years of operations through reduced irrigation (water) costs, even with the requirement that the good bacteria would need to be reintroduced every thirty years. He encouraged us to do the math to verify his claims; our team monitored the irrigation needs of the test garden and saw that it needed 50 percent of the water we had anticipated. We calculated that the soil improvements would indeed pay for themselves several times over during each of the thirty-year lifespans of the good bacteria, and worked to reallocate the project's construction and operating budgets to take this new information into account.

By the time the royal family came to inspect the building and garden mock-up, everything was finished, installed, and thriving, and their satisfaction with the garden helped in our presentation of the revised budget with higher costs for initial soil improvements offset by lower annual irrigation costs. Their visit was a complete success, so much so that they insisted on keeping the mock-up building intact as part of the future beach palace complex. Instead of demolishing it, the bedroom and balcony remained and can be seen to this day.

Behind the Scenes with Our Team in This Project's "Delivery Room"

The success of this project was remarkable, especially when you consider the fact that we were a team charged with creating an exotic garden and our first very run-of-the-mill test garden died after only four weeks. Our PhD expert was a godsend, and his focus on solutions and ability to understand our need to stay within our budget was a refreshing quality to find in a scientist. The inspection by the royal family couldn't have gone better, and we even got to see our initial mock-up become part of the permanent palace complex. Everything looks perfect, right?

Well, in fact, as in almost every real-world construction project, even a "perfect" outcome is only achieved after several bumps along the road to completion. In this case, finding a creative technical solution offset several issues in our "delivery room" that could have become problems and doomed our project. First, the introduction of a mock-up in any project creates the risk that once an issue is discovered, the characters in the delivery room will focus more on shifting blame and liability to others instead of collaborating to find a solution. This project was particularly vulnerable to this type of difficulty. For one thing, the owner is the country's royal family, and no one wants to be responsible for delivering anything below their expectations. Second, and related to this first point because they *are* the royal family, their desire for a spectacular seaside garden raised the stakes for our project team's landscaping professionals. The unique soil and irrigation considerations of the site weren't at all suited for the specified plants and trees. The fact that the specified olive trees were one thousand years old and imported from Spain only made the need to get things right even more urgent. Just about any landscaping professional would be tested beyond their skills, and the fact that our landscapers were part of the contractor's team further complicated our delivery room team dynamics.

The designer/doctor specified exotic and expensive plants and trees because that was what the owner (in this case, the royal family) wanted. The designer didn't fully understand the complexities of the site, nor did they anticipate the fact that most landscapers in Qatar weren't up to the challenge of implementing a design that would keep one thousand-year-old trees from Spain alive. I knew that as the project manager, I was potentially opening a can of worms with my mock-up of the garden, but also knew that things would be far worse if we simply waited until the actual garden was installed to see if it would, in fact, survive. One dead one thousand-year-old Spanish olive tree would certainly be one too many.

Illustration: 1,000-year-old olive trees purchased from Spain and transported to Qatar to be planted in the project. They survived the harsh weather thanks to the bio-treatment proposed by a consultant recruited by the project manager.

Our contractor's landscaping professional was smart enough to know there would be special challenges at our beach palace location and was happy to conduct an initial test planting. They expected it to fail, or at least knew there was a significant chance it might, so they were also ready to propose a consultation by the PhD expert to get to a solution. The technical solution our team discovered with this expert's help was only part of the answer, however. The contractor themselves would have to implement the expert's solution and warrant its performance, and the consultant would also have to supervise the new solution and warrant that it would work as part of their design as well. Each of these characters would need to adjust not only to the new solution that would allow the garden to "perform" as designed, but also to accept their originally-agreed liability for their role in the design (consultant) and construction (contractor) of the garden with its new soil and irrigation system. Further, as the project manager, I would have the pleasure of introducing a new budget to the royal family to convince them that long-term savings in their operating budget would offset higher construction costs.

It all took the sort of choreography of implementing a promising solution that faces every successful project manager. First, I needed to identify the character with the highest motivation for finding a solution to the issue of a grove of dead one thousand-year-old olive trees. That would be the contractor, since it would be easier for the designer to blame them for faulty implementation of their specifications than to accept responsibility for improper design. So I began discussing my plan for engaging the French expert with the contractor before any other character. After all, it was their landscaping professional who saw the issue in the first place, and who acted in the way a successful team member should act when they suggested a solution at the time the issue first arose.

Once the contractor agreed, I could then approach the designer to invite them to participate in the creation of a new mock-up garden based on the expert's proposal. It helped that the expert was highly convincing and seemed eminently qualified. It also helped that I went to his research facility, which was in the same country and had similar soil conditions, to verify that he could, in fact, do what he said. I could use this visit to vouch for the expert's solution, which reduced the likelihood that one of the existing team members—the designer, most probably—would introduce another counterproposal, creating a time-consuming test of alternatives that might have been based simply on efforts to shift liability instead of looking for an effective solution.

The designer agreed with my recommendation, as supported by the contractor, that we test the PhD expert's proposed solution. But this agreement came with the condition that the test be conducted under the joint supervision of the contractor and the designer. This was not a difficult condition to accept, although to be honest none of us were 100 percent sure that the PhD expert's promises would be realized. None of us had a PhD in botany, after all. But because a properly conducted mock-up would yield objective results, and because our project schedule allowed time for this new mock-up, we could move forward as a team and watch the new garden survive and thrive. Sometimes solutions do grow on trees.

A Final Observation: The Unexpected Benefits of Our Expert's Solution

As mentioned earlier in this chapter, the budget was unlikely to be a serious concern for this particular owner. Money is usually no object when a royal family wants to construct a summer palace for its own enjoyment. Our team's concern was much more serious when it came to the question of whether the garden would survive over time, since being responsible for the displeasure of a king is never a good thing for anyone.

Our team could have stopped when it came to introducing the expert's "good" bacteria to sweeten the soil in the royal family's gardens, ignoring the expert's second recommendation to add volcanic rock to save water and reduce irrigation costs. In a project whose owner did not have access to an unlimited budget, this wouldn't be possible, but this time it was. We chose to accept the proposal for introducing volcanic rock and, in the process, create a project that was more environmentally sustainable. We were proud to be "green," and were happy to tell the royal family that they would not only be saving money in annual irrigation costs, but they would also be doing something that would conserve natural resources. It was heartening to see how pleased they were, and to share this additional benefit of our team's solution with them.

My belief as a project manager is that if I can find a solution to an issue that is economically viable, one that performs at least as well as the project's original design specifications, and that meets all code and government regulations, there is sometimes an opportunity to do more.

Sometimes it is a kind of artistic achievement in executing a beautiful design; at other times it is bringing new economic opportunities to a community when a new hotel opens and hires residents, or a shopping mall becomes home to new businesses owned by a city's entrepreneurs. In this case, we could find a solution that saved water, one of the earth's most precious natural resources.

In the not-too-distant future, considerations about the availability of water, and ideas for how to save or even recycle water as part of a project's design and construction, will be one of the most important measures of its success. The answers we found for a challenge seemingly so remote—keeping one thousand-year-old olive trees alive along the coast of Qatar in a palace garden—are exciting to me because the need for more sweet soil and more efficient use of irrigation water can be answered by applying the same ideas and systems we implemented in the royal family's garden. Sharing this solution in a way that goes beyond the creation of a beautiful landscape to the maintenance of habitable communities or reduction of conflicts over access to freshwater has benefits far beyond a single construction project.

Today, the military conflict in Syria, Iraq, and the Middle East affects the ability of citizens to access freshwater, along with the quality of water that is available from the Degla and Furat Rivers. Similar geopolitical and water quality issues can be found in the Nile River Valley as it passes through Egypt and Ethiopia. In America, western states are struggling with each other about the rights to dam rivers that flow through one to another.

We've all read forecasts by environmentalists and economists that today's wars over oil may one day be replaced by wars fought about water. The 2015 Expo in Milan, Italy, was dedicated to the topic of agriculture and the idea that the future world may face crises about the availability of food and other resources that will need real-world solutions. What is exciting about our work in construction projects is that many techniques that may one day help find answers to the challenge of feeding the world's population, or guaranteeing the human right to water, are already available to us on a small scale in each of our projects. If we're lucky, we can sometimes take a step back from our regular concern with keeping our work on schedule, within budget, and consistent with performance standards, to thoughts of how the solutions we find and implement in constructing a new building or creating the support systems that keep it sustainable over time can have a larger meaning.

If we're lucky, sometimes while we act on a small scale, measured in square meters, we can also dream in larger terms that are measured in the quality of human lives.

Chapter Six
It's Academic—Creative Ideas from the Project Teams of Tomorrow

Illustrations: Scenes from the multidisciplinary training program in Qatar, bringing together students and project professionals to propose, study, and test new technologies and practices for future implementation.

Chapter Six
It's Academic—Creative Ideas from the Project Teams of Tomorrow

In closing the last chapter, I touched on the importance of project managers looking for ways to use the knowledge gained in work to address important challenges the world will face in the future. Looming shortages of food and water are global problems, and the techniques we use to meet budget and performance standards on a micro level can have an impact if they are aggregated into best practices that can be incorporated into many other projects. Reducing the need for consumption of resources like water and energy, finding ways to source materials locally to lower costs (and energy consumption) associated with shipping components from faraway factories, and recycling waste to transform it into resources that can be used on site are some of the solutions my teams and I have researched, tested, and implemented to solve issues that have arisen during virtually all the projects with which I've been associated.

In several of the examples illustrated so far, I've described ways we've solved issues in real time—as members of our team have discovered them. In a few cases, I've introduced the value of tests and mock-ups as a technique to probe for possible solutions to issues that might arise on a large scale by creating an early, smaller-scale model of possible sensitive or uncertain elements of the entire project. I believe in the value of mock-ups, because they allow us to "solve tomorrow's issues today," while the risks in terms of time and budget resources are much lower. But there is another way, and that is to engage young people—students and fresh graduates with degrees in design, engineering, management, and other disciplines—in today's projects, so they can gain valuable experience that will enable them to anticipate tomorrow's challenges by exposing them to real issues in active projects. Health professionals often bring medical residents into hospitals, health centers, and, yes, delivery rooms so they can observe and learn the actual practice of medicine. I believe this same technique is extremely valuable on project sites, and am happy to report that it can be done.

With the support of senior management, my company created an eight-week training program for students from many world-class universities to participate in one of our signature projects. Students came from the electrical and mechanical engineering programs at Texas A&M University's Doha Branch in Qatar; from the interior design program at Virginia Commonwealth University, also from its Doha, Qatar, branch; and the engineering and architecture programs at Qatar University. They gathered for a summer on the site where we were constructing the St. Regis Hotel Qatar in Doha—the first St. Regis Hotel to be built in the Middle East. An iconic hospitality project would give students from different disciplines a chance to contribute their individual talents to the success of the project while they could benefit from being together and sharing their experiences in looking for innovative solutions to the multiple issues we challenged them to study and solve.

The St. Regis Qatar Hotel project was designed to be a high-end destination with three hundred and forty hotel rooms, another four hundred fully serviced apartments, and associated amenities including food services, retail areas, and recreation centers totaling three hundred and fifty thousand square meters in built-up area. It would be billed as "the finest address in Qatar," combining the guest experience and corporate standards of the St. Regis brand with respect for the values and culture of Qatar and the Middle East. For the students in our program, the project would also include the challenge of making everything comply with the United States Green Building Council (USGBC) Leadership in Energy and Environmental Design (LEED) standards. These standards are one of the world's most popular programs for designing buildings, homes, and communities in environmentally responsible ways, so their construction, operation, and maintenance can use resources efficiently.

Illustration: A schematic drawing of the St. Regis Qatar Hotel project.

The Qatar University Project Team Training Program

Our training program included four elements:

1. Students from each discipline studied design drawings and specifications.
2. They observed construction on site and learned how actual work compares and contrasts with design documents.
3. They studied LEED standards for green buildings and worked with our team to select project components where their skills and expertise matched opportunities to make the project more compliant with LEED.

4. They proposed enhancements to our project's design, construction methods, specification of materials and components, and other elements to achieve specific LEED standards.

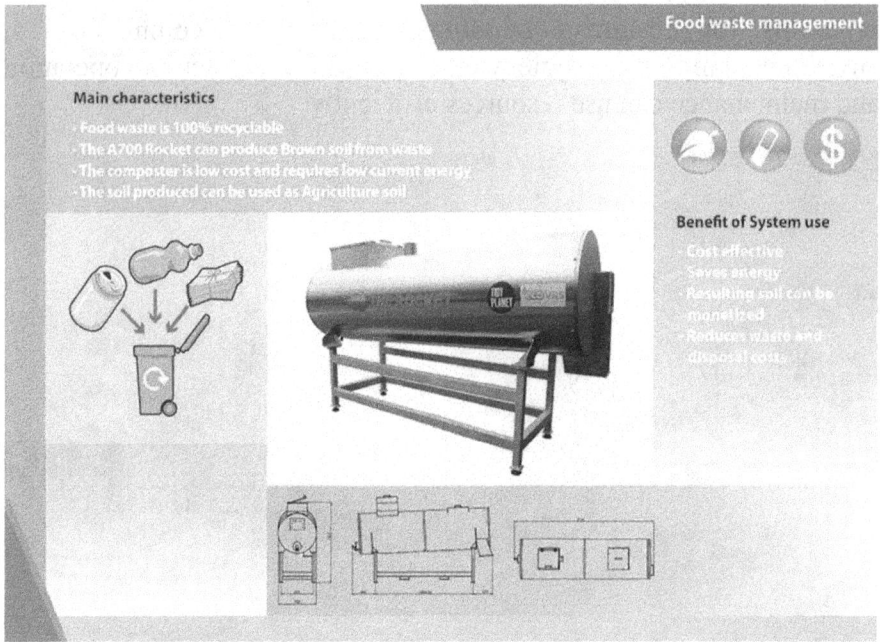

Illustration: A supplier schematic of the food waste compactor system.

During the program, our student project team members contributed remarkably creative ideas in six areas of the new St. Regis Qatar Hotel. Following is a summary of each of them:

1. Food service. This is a huge area of the St. Regis hotel and residential apartment complex, with more than two thousand employees. The hotel complex's food services would generate a great amount of waste, which would need to be stored prior to removal at a temperature no greater than eight degrees Celsius to prevent the growth of dangerous bacteria. Our students considered the project's original design, LEED standards, and possible solutions and came up with a compactor system that handles 100 percent of the area's food waste. The innovative aspect of this

system is that, running on low current electricity, it treats the waste so that over a two-week period, it transforms it into rich, sweet soil suitable for planting and use in exterior landscaping. This soil could therefore be used for the site's own landscaping needs once the system was installed and in use and, after that, the sweet soil generated by the waste compactor would be available for the hotel to sell and earn revenue.

2. Local sourcing. When a project involves a large international corporation as the owner, materials are typically specified so they give the owner comfort and reassurance that they will meet performance and quality standards. This was certainly the case with the St. Regis Corporation, and our team's contractor selected branded materials and components from vendors in the United States and Europe. The costs of these materials were therefore significantly increased when shipping costs were added in, and the use of these distant suppliers also diminished the project's ability to adjust to changing circumstances and needs due to the time it would take to send things from hundreds or thousands of miles away. Materials that did not arrive at precisely the right time would incur costs beyond those associated with shipping alone. If they arrived too late, there would be delays, which would bring additional costs such as the need to continue to pay construction workers while they were idle. If they arrived too early, we would need to pay to store these materials until they were needed.

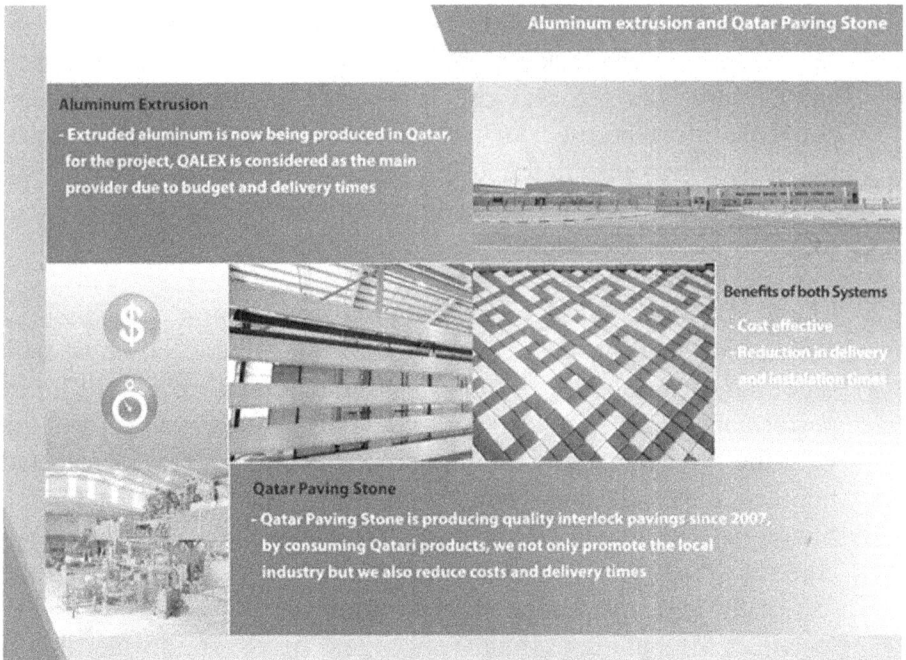

Illustration: A supplier schematic showing the benefits of using locally sourced interlocking paving stones.

Our students found two solutions to save our project significant amounts of money and eliminate the energy costs associated with long-distance shipping. The first was the use of locally sourced interlocking paving stones instead of asphalt or concrete for the project's streets and sidewalks. These stones were produced in Qatar, and their total cost—once shipping was included—was lower than either alternative solution. There was also an additional benefit to this idea, since the appearance of the interlocking stones gave the project an image of luxury and quality that the owners appreciated, while performing equally well or better than concrete or asphalt.

The second solution was a bit more complex and more of a macroeconomic program than one to serve our project alone. The St. Regis project called for aluminum windows, requiring the fabrication of these custom-designed pieces at a factory capable of extruding these forms from aluminum cylinders using dies and high heat. Once the aluminum forms were cut to shape to fit the hotel's various window sizes, the factory would also be responsible for adding glass and shipping the finished windows to our site for installation. It would be "normal" for us to go to a factory in the United States or Germany for this work, which was expensive in terms of fabrication costs alone, before the addition of significant shipping expenses.

Our students' solution was to source a quality extrusion factory in Qatar. In fact, a new extrusion factory had just been commissioned, making it possible to purchase the desired materials. The savings associated with shipping finished windows over a distance of a few miles instead of several thousand miles was substantial, to say the least. And because Qatar has a booming economy, the demand for similar windows for other local projects was a primary reason for constructing the local extrusion factory.

Toilet for disabled

Main characteristics
- HEWI's 01 system integrates it's elements into a single surface wall
- It uses "push release" mechanisms to easily open accesories
- Non-contact flushing mechanisms
- Wash basins and urinals are also available

Main features

- Wall mounted fittings	- Paper towel dispenser	- Hinged support rails
- Mirror	- Soap dispenser	- Paper towel basque
- Shelf	- Toilet paper holder	- Privacy screens
- Toilet brush unit	- Spare roll holder	- Hook

Illustration: Supplier schematic showing installation of ADA-compliant toilet systems that eliminate the need for separate facilities.

3. Toilet for the Disabled. Public restroom design for disabled people is best described as functional, not luxurious. There are usually small basic stalls in a row alongside a larger stall equipped with utilitarian handrails and open space. Our students found a commercially available system that integrates all features necessary for use by disabled people into a single design that can be used by anyone. A single surface wall holds accessories such as paper towel dispenser, soap dispenser, toilet paper holder, and hinged support rails. These are designed to be accessible via push release mechanisms so the user can select the accessories they want while allowing the others to remain retracted and invisible. Toilets have noncontact flushing mechanisms, and similar proximity sensors operate the faucets of the units' hand washing sinks. The system also includes washbasins and urinals in alternative designs. The fact that each unit is the same eliminates the need to designate some of them for disabled use only, making the restrooms more welcoming for all, and the use of retractable features and accessories allows for the more luxurious look the St. Regis wanted in their hotel.

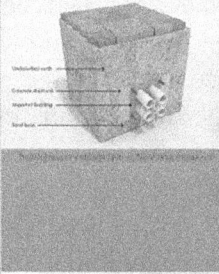

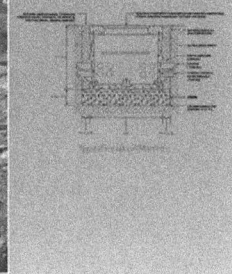

Illustration: Supplier schematic showing long-distance electrical wiring duct systems allowing for improved aesthetics, installation, and maintenance.

4. Electrical Wiring Infrastructure. The hotel complex was designed to include five separate towers. Two are for the hotel, two more for larger apartments of two, three, or five bedrooms, and a fifth tower is single apartments—either studios or one-bedroom units. This design is in keeping with Middle Eastern values, which discourage mixing families with bachelors in the same building. To provide electricity to these separate towers using conventional underground cables, there would need to be manhole access every thirty meters. Distances longer than this would cause too much resistance to pulling the cables out for maintenance and repairs. The St. Regis owners believed that a manhole every thirty meters would disrupt their exterior design standards, and were looking for a way to reduce this need. The answer our students found was to use a trench duct that could handle multiple wires, and protected each wire with its own durable "pipe" to allow pulling of individual wires over distances much greater than the thirty-meter maximum

length required for standard design. This solution also demonstrated the synergy possible by encouraging students from different disciplines to collaborate on the project: because the site would be paved with interlocking stones that are more "forgiving" than paving with asphalt or concrete, the trench could be wider than standard cabling trenches, reducing the time and cost of installation. The use of multiple individual wires in protective pipes also reduced the cost of maintenance because the space between each wire and its pipe allowed longer pulling for repairs. And in the unlikely event that a wire might need to be repaired by digging through the project's paved roads and sidewalks above the wires, the interlocking stone design would also make accessing the wire an easier process, and replacing the stones would maintain the overall look and feel of the roadway more effectively than cutting and replacing asphalt or poured concrete.

Illustration: Hollow core slabs manufactured in nearby facilities can dramatically improve project cost, time, and quality standards.

5. Hollow Core Slab. The project's original design called for the use of reinforced poured concrete for the building's walls. This is a lengthy process, requiring twenty-one days. It involves assembling a form, or tray, into which steel bars are placed, followed by the pouring of concrete to fill the tray. It takes three weeks to dry, after which the finished concrete wall is ready for use and the tray is ready for use in constructing another wall. Materials are inexpensive, and there is a good deal of flexibility in maintaining an adequate supply if the project schedule accelerates—if there are enough forms to construct walls so a constant number of "new" ones are available after curing for twenty-one days. But, consistent with our experience working with our student team members, they found a better alternative: hollow core slabs prefabricated in advance in a nearby factory. This was not as obvious a solution as it might seem: the factory-produced slabs are normally more expensive than poured reinforced concrete. But in this case, because the project was so large, the factory could create a manufacturing process that provided economy of scale. They grouped together the number of identically sized slabs and created a gigantic form that could produce ten of them at once, cutting this enormous slab into ten equal pieces. While the initial fixed costs of this fabrication method were high, it turned out that the cost *per slab* would be lower than pouring concrete on the project site. It took a thorough analysis of the project's requirements and a corresponding look at the factory's capabilities in terms of interior space (could it hold the gigantic form that made ten slabs at once?) and production capacity (could it produce enough slabs to meet the project's demands?). Once our students were satisfied that these were possible, they recommended going forward with this innovative and lower-cost alternative.

Illustration: Treating water from sinks in residential and public areas in reverse osmosis systems for irrigation and other nonhuman-consumption purposes offer exciting opportunities for environmentally sound, cost-effective operations.

6. **Reuse of Water for Building Systems.** Our final example of student contributions to the environmentally responsible construction and operation of the St. Regis Qatar Hotel involved ways to reduce the demand for freshwater during its daily operations. In talks with our team, students learned that the demand for water within the buildings themselves—drinking and bathing by guests and residents, use in the preparation of food, and cleaning operations of various kinds—was high. In cold weather, this use is between one hundred and fifty and two hundred liters per person per day. In hot weather, it can climb to two hundred and fifty to three hundred liters per person per day. When additional requirements for water, such as irrigation in landscaping, the hotel's pools, and other amenities are added, the students were concerned about whether these collective demands may be large enough to exceed the capacity of the site to supply an adequate amount of freshwater.

Our students' solution was twofold. First, it involved the use of reverse osmosis wastewater treatment systems to treat water from selected sources—such as guests' and residents' sinks. Second, it further involved management of this treated water so it is not used for drinking but is used in other ways, such as flushing toilets or irrigation of exterior landscaping areas. This plan can save significant amounts of water for treatment and reuse without risking the health of guests and residents. They will continue their access to freshwater for regular use and bathing, while uses that do not involve their consumption of water can use recycled water treated by the site's new reverse osmosis treatment systems.

* * * * *

The benefits these students contributed to our St. Regis Hotel project are summarized in these six examples; they will all help the project move closer to LEED certification and in the process, will achieve performance standards that conserve resources and reduce stresses on the environment. But these are not the only benefits of this program: the students who participated learned professional skills and project management practices that will contribute to their future success as designers, engineers, project managers, and professionals in other fields. Future programs with other schools, which can be located anywhere in the world, will continue to provide these opportunities for other students. Innovations like the Qatar Foundation's Hub of Top International Universities Project Team Training Program allow students to learn via observation, via mentoring by seasoned professionals in their field, and via trial-and-error exploration of solutions for real on-site issues. They open the door for the chance to make real contributions while they advance their studies, and in the process they gain the confidence that can only be learned by finding out that, in fact, they can do the work involved in the career they have chosen for themselves.

Closing Thoughts from an Experienced Project Manager

Creating a program in which the project teams of tomorrow can practice their skills in the real world while they contribute solutions to the kinds of issues they will soon face in their own careers is something that moves me to serious reflections on the importance of education, the world's growing need for talented and successful project managers, and the contributions our profession can make in solving some of the most significant challenges the future will bring. But beyond that, it also makes me think of who we are as human beings, why we exist, and what kinds of wealth we amass and share during our lives. It's that important to me, and I hope you will agree that it is something that is equally important for all of us.

When my teams and I discover an issue that requires a solution to maintain our success, I think about how, as a single individual, I need to divide myself in a sense, in order to accomplish tasks that are related but different from each other. I must become an investigator to gather knowledge and look for possible solutions. I must become a leader to deliver this knowledge to other members of my team to gain their understanding and support for the solution I believe will work. And I must also be an executive to transform this knowledge into effective action that solves the issue.

In doing these things—all the elements that contribute to the successful performance of my project management responsibilities—my team and I create wealth. It is wealth we can observe—a beautiful new building that functions as designed; and it is wealth we can measure—the financial rewards that accrue to everyone involved in a successful project. These kinds of wealth are what I call "fixed" wealth. They are things, and can be measured in physical ways.

But there is also a second kind of wealth that I believe is even more important. It is "moving wealth"—in other words, the resource of the human being—or the kind of value that is involved in creating a building, paving a road, designing an environmentally efficient irrigation system, or writing a book. Creating this moving wealth is also something we do as human beings, and it involves dividing ourselves in yet another way. We become teachers; we share information with others, perhaps younger people we hope will one day become the project managers, the architects, the contractors, or even the teachers of tomorrow. We create moving wealth by sharing, not by gathering. And despite all the beautiful buildings my teams and I have created during my career, I am more proud of having created moving wealth than I am of any physical project.

Chapter Seven
Conclusion

Chapter Seven
Conclusion

Looking back on the case studies that make up chapters two through five—the boundary wall that had been forgotten in the construction schedule in chapter two; the need for a simple gravity-fed wastewater disposal system in chapter three; the switch from use of reinforced concrete to prefabricated lightweight steel and fiber cement board structures in chapter four; and the creation of a unique landscaping soil based on a PhD expert's recommendation in chapter five—we saw how the characters on a construction project team acted in a remarkably similar way to how expecting parents and their medical team work together in the delivery room. This same analogy also held in the six additional project ideas introduced by design and engineering students in chapter six. In all cases, the project benefited from the theoretical and academic skills of the designer (or doctor, in the delivery room); the committed effort of the contractor and their team of construction workers (or mother); the intense concern and willingness to do whatever it takes by the owner (or father); and the ability to assess the situation in real time and keep the entire team moving together toward successful completion by the project manager (or nurse).

The fact is that even when issues arise and one or more of these characters act in a way that seems counterproductive, or let emotions get the best of logical thinking, a successful project needs all of them working together as a team to be successful. A skilled and experienced project manager knows this, and is therefore as interested in managing the relationships among team members as they are in the technical aspects of any individual issue that arises during the project schedule. Note that this focus on relationships doesn't mean failing to pay attention to technical concerns—far from it. As we will discuss at the end of this chapter, the proper use of technical knowledge is an essential way to manage a construction project team. But more about this later....

Remember also my point in the previous chapter about the distinction between fixed and moving wealth. Fixed wealth—buildings, roads, automobiles, clothes, etc.—are man-made. But moving wealth—the technical knowledge and management skills that can be found within the human mind and are required to build anything classified as fixed wealth—is God-made. It is this moving wealth that keeps the real goal of a construction project at the forefront of the team's attention. As they build it stone by stone, or wire by wire, or interior finish by interior finish, there is always the overall purpose of the project and each of its component structures and systems that governs the success or failure of these individual elements. No project can ever succeed without the diligent and consistent application of moving wealth. It is the team that puts together the project that is always the most important thing; it is never the project itself. A successful project manager always understands the fact that focusing on the team is their most important job.

Doing this requires a specific mindset on the part of the project manager, and—most often—the ability to transfer this same mindset to key members of the project team. It is a mindset that is not as afraid to make mistakes, as it is willing to learn from the damages caused by these errors. It is a mindset that depends on the human brain—or even better, a collection of human brains—to find corrective action in response to mistakes. A collection of human brains is optimal because, as we have seen repeatedly in the examples in this book, integrated solutions built on the expertise and ideas of multiple team members are almost always better than the idea of a single team member. Theoretical designs, whether they are implemented directly from the project designer or adapted through the introduction of additional ideas from outside experts, are always made better by the contractor that builds them, and through the timely approval and support of the owner. The project manager is the one individual on the project who always understands the value of this type of synergy. Keeping the team together in a way that maintains their collective positive frame of mind, their enjoyment of the process of working together, and their commitment to never admit there are problems but always focus on issues and solutions—this is the role of the project manager. Successful project managers create teams, not projects.

Project Review Checklist

We'll conclude this book with a short checklist of key things a project manager would do well to remember at the beginning of every construction project. They're organized—not surprisingly—into two main categories: "fixed wealth" and "moving wealth." Within each category are several questions based on the stories in this book, along with spaces for other questions that might arise based on the unique characteristics of a new project. Similarly, the questions based on chapters of this book may or may not apply to another project based on those same specifics. In some cases, one or more of these checklist items may not be present in a project that is successful. In other cases, all items on the checklist may be present but some of them might not be answered in an optimal way. These are all possible outcomes in individual construction projects and, during a long career, you will probably see any number of differences in terms of boxes checked. But in more cases than not, remembering this checklist can be a valuable place to begin making sure key aspects are planned and considered as every project takes shape. Eventually, you'll remember the categories in which the questions are organized more than the questions themselves: fixed vs. moving wealth, followed by subcategories like walls and structural systems, water management, etc. (fixed wealth); and imagination, timing, issues never problems, etc. (moving wealth). The checklist follows:

Project Review Check List

At the beginning of every project, the thorough review I have recommended in a number of previous chapters must take place, and it is recommended to organize this review from the points of view outlined below. Note that a number of these are specific to the projects we have discussed in this book. Future projects may require different technical review criteria based on their own unique characteristics, but it is my belief that many of these same technical criteria apply to a majority of construction projects.

Fixed Wealth (Technical) Questions for My Project

1. Walls and Structural Systems

   - Does this project use lightweight steel structures?
   - Does this project use fiber cement board?
   - Does this project use hollow core slabs?
   - What is the *maximum* bearing load capacity of the soil?
   - How does the building loading compare to this capacity?
   - Are subcontractors calling for any changes in specifications?
   - Other walls and structural systems questions.

2. Water Management

   - Does this project require a vacuum wastewater system?
   - Does this project use bacteria enhancement for sweet soil?
   - Is there a need to reduce the amount of irrigation water?
   - Does the level of water consumption need to be managed?
   - Has reuse of wastewater from sinks been considered?
   - Is there a need for a reverse osmosis plant?
   - Are subcontractors calling for any changes in specifications?
   - Other water management questions.

3. Electromechanical Systems

- What is the projected number of manholes on internal roads?
- Will proposed electrical wires on site be buried or ducted?
- Are subcontractors calling for any changes in specifications?
- Other electromechanical systems questions.

4. Other Technical Systems

- Have contractors submitted procurement logs for materials procured within 100 miles? Beyond 100 miles?
- Will the project use ADA toilets that can be integrated into the design of normal toilets?
- Are subcontractors calling for any changes in specifications?
- Additional questions about other technical systems.

Moving Wealth Questions for My Project

1. Anticipation and Imagination

- What are the "gray areas" in the project's design documents?
- Can you imagine what might be needed to solve these issues?
- Does the project's timetable ensure success?
- Can adjusting the schedule avoid delays or other issues?
- Is the project team complete in terms of skills and talents?
- What are possible sources for skills that are missing?
- Have you identified where tests and mock-ups can be used?
- Additional questions about pre-project planning.

2. Focus on Issues, Not Problems

- Does the team understand that there are issues, not problems?
- Is it understood that issues are never discussed without possible solutions?
- Are sources of additional skills and resources always available?
- Additional questions about solving issues as they arise.

3. The Importance of Knowledge and Prioritization of Values

    *   Is the project team committed to relying on technical knowledge to solve issues?
    *   Who is responsible for providing necessary technical knowledge?
    *   Are changes in the project's anticipated schedule, cost, and quality being monitored?
    *   How are these changes used to adjust project management priorities?
    *   Is it always clear that time is the most important value?
    *   Additional questions about knowledge and values.

Suggestions for conducting the project's initial fixed and moving wealth review:

As noted at the beginning of this chapter, the checklist provided on the previous pages is intended to help readers develop their own approach to reviewing a new project's requirements for management of technical issues (fixed wealth) and management of the project team (moving wealth). Because each new project will always be unique, it is important to take a flexible approach to this process. To help readers develop such an approach, following are a few conceptual priorities to remember:

Part One: The Importance of Anticipation and Imagination

To ensure a project's success, several steps can be taken early in the life of a project team, before work commences.

1. Take an imaginative look at the project on paper. Study the design documents to see where you are confident there won't be issues with key aspects, and on the other hand, where there are items that seem incomplete or subject to better possible solutions. These can be site-specific matters like a choice of construction methods or selecting different electrical or wastewater disposal systems; or they can be based on more global concerns like recycling to save water, or using more energy-efficient technologies. There are many

Yasser Osman Ph.D., PMP. & Yara Osman

possibilities; the point is that at the beginning of the project, use your imagination.

2. Anticipate the timing of the project. As you use your imagination about which elements of the project might need different solutions or ideas, also think about how the project schedule will unfold. As we've seen in a few of our case studies, some of the issues that threaten a project's success result from doing one thing too early, or forgetting to finish all preliminary steps before advancing to final construction. Comedians say that timing is everything. So do successful project managers.

3. Learn to manage the team you need, not the one you have. It's not always possible for the project manager to select key project team members. For example, the owner is already in place by the time the project is initiated, and the designer's work has also been completed. But a complex construction project requires a project manager who can manage these other key project team "characters." In other words, make sure you get to know the unique characteristics of other team members. How do they interact with others on the site? Are they team players, or does one or more of them seem to function better on their own? Do they have the technical skills required for the project, or are there areas where the team could use additional professionals in order to manage issues that may arise? In my experience, it helps to draw an extended organizational chart to identify key members and identify the skills and talents they have. Next, create a second chart of skills required for the project. Does the team have all the required skills within it? Are there any skills that are lacking? By doing this, a project manager can consider ways to add these skills to the team in advance. There are always suppliers or subcontractors with these skills and talents, and it is better to add these members to a team at the beginning of the project instead of waiting for an issue to develop once work is underway. Addressing issues in advance is one of the major benefits of an imaginative review of the design documents.

4. Share issues with your project team in advance. It's never too early to look for solutions to issues that will arise during a project.

Anticipating them and realizing where creative solutions might be possible is an important responsibility for every successful project manager. Talking about them with your team can lead to any number of possible solutions.

5. Make the project as real as possible, as early as possible. This book includes several examples of my teams and me using mock-ups or tests of possible solutions in order to solve issues in a timely and successful way. Real-life examples of how a proposed solution might work are far more valuable than theoretical discussions of whether these solutions might work. Use tests and mock-ups whenever possible.

Part Two: A Focus on Issues, Not Problems ... Leads to Success, Not Failure.

Despite a project team's best effort, it is not possible to anticipate every issue that will arise during the life of a project. Managing these issues effectively requires the same creativity and team management skills required in advance of a project's start date, along with additional qualities, such as a relentlessly positive attitude, a belief in the abilities of a project team, and a willingness to bring additional skills and resources to the worksite if they are necessary.

6. Remember the importance of stressing that there are issues, never problems. Issues have solutions; problems do not. Discuss the rule I have enforced with my teams that the word "problem" is banned from our management discussions, unless there is a truly fatal accident. And remember the secondary rule that no team member can bring an issue to the rest of the team without suggesting a possible solution or at least introducing a strategy for finding a successful solution for the issue.

7. When an issue arises, don't wait. Look for solutions as soon as possible. Sometimes, even with the best imaginative review of design documents or the most thorough efforts to anticipate every possible issue, an issue still arises in the middle of an otherwise routine project. When it happens, remember that the best way to

keep the team together, and to keep everyone in a positive frame of mind, is to begin work immediately on solving the issue. Engage the team, beginning with the team member who brought the problem to everyone's attention in the first place. Don't be afraid to keep the conversation going even if there's no obvious solution. Creative teamwork is the only way to succeed when dealing with unforeseen issues.

8. Know who to ask. A corollary of not waiting to solve an issue when it arises is knowing who to ask. As noted above, start with the team member who brings the issue to your attention in the first place. That's the rule we want to enforce, after all. But sometimes this person really can't propose a good solution, and when that happens, it's up to the project manager to keep things moving forward. The next place to look for a possible solution is the rest of the team. If the contractor discovers the issue, bring it to the attention of the designer and the owner. If the members of your current team strike out, don't stop there. Go to outside people associated with the project team. For example, maybe there are specialty subcontractors hired by the contractor, or the owner, or even the design team. Maybe one of these individuals or companies can solve the issue, and your team members should feel comfortable bringing their skills to the attention of the rest of the team. It's part of the overall positive team mindset a good project manager creates and maintains. Finally, if all else fails, bring in an expert. Remember our French botanist who recommended the introduction of good bacteria and lava rocks for landscaping the Qatari royal family's beach palace? It worked for us. Maybe another expert will work for you.

Part Three: The Importance of Focusing on Knowledge and Value.

People often ask me to tell them what aspects of project management are the most critical to success. I have learned to be careful in answering such questions, because each project is unique, and what makes one project succeed is just a minor detail in many other projects. However, there are two general categories I can honestly say are almost always required for a project manager to be successful in every project. One is the ability to use technical knowledge in developing and promoting solutions for issues that arise. And a second is an understanding of which elements of a project's key values—time, cost, and quality—deserve the highest priority.

9. Focus on knowledge. At the beginning of the conclusion, I mentioned the importance of the project manager focusing on managing the team and not on trying to solve technical issues on their own. I believe this sincerely, but I also believe in the importance of relying on technical knowledge to evaluate the potential for a proposed solution to resolve the issue at hand. The reliance on technical information is so valuable to project managers that I almost think of it as a trick, or at least a secret weapon. When issues arise on a project, team members often retreat to conversations about budget issues, or about the schedule. They argue about these topics because they are subjects everyone on the team can claim as being within their own experience. But when it comes to technical issues, I have found that most project team members shy away from talking about them. They either don't know enough to engage in a detailed conversation, or they agree that an expert might help the entire team evaluate the most current and accurate information about this technical subject. I have always won arguments when I have engaged in them about technical subjects. You can, too.

10. Define value as a combination of the following factors *in a consistent order of priority*: time, then cost, and then quality. In many cases, we look for a priority among these three parameters based on the specifics of each project, and in doing so confuses the importance of all three of them. Based on my experience, I believe that time is always the number one priority in projects; if we deliver the project partially or fully on time and allow for the client to use his building partially or fully as soon as possible, we can always justify additional costs and variance in quality. This is because a project that is at least partially completed is already able to at least partially earn revenue that can be channeled to support

continued construction. Going back to the very beginning of this book and the analogy of the Delivery Room, we also found the importance of on-time delivery: a baby will not survive if it remains six months beyond the deadline of nine months; and it will also be in serious jeopardy if delivered sooner than this same nine-month schedule. To conclude, I would like readers to keep in mind that the ***definition of value always equals Time, Time, and always Time first, followed by Cost and Quality.***

As a final thought, I want to express my solidarity with project managers, wherever in the world you may be working, and whatever the stage of your career. To young project managers, I say welcome. To those with experience, I say not only thank you, but I encourage you to lend more of your time to teaching those who will follow. And to all of us, I want to stress the value of our work in putting real solutions in place to solve problems that work on the scale of an individual project. But in many cases, as I will always remember from my experiences at events like the Milan Expo in 2015, our solutions have much larger potential to solve problems on a global scale. It's what makes me want to go to work every day, and what makes me look forward to the next project in my career. Thanks for reading, and good luck to all of you!

About the Authors

Dr. Yasser Osman has a distinguished background in the planning, design, and program/construction management of several unique, large scale projects. He represented EWH to develop their new hospital, the first St. Regis in the Middle East, along with notable projects in the US and other countries. He was involved in leading the expansion of the healthcare system with new branches, and oversaw the transition of the company into a publicly traded business entity. When he is not involved in expansion, he manages the renovation and expansion of existing buildings, often with historic significance. He is familiar with a variety of project delivery methods, from traditional design-bid-build to design-build; well versed in program management; and has a keen eye for schedule and cost control. Well respected by clients and colleagues, Dr. Osman is known for establishing and maintaining excellent communication across multidisciplines, such as design teams, project stakeholders, owners, and contractors. He can be reached via his LinkedIn account at https://www.linkedin.com/in/yasser-osman-a4234934/.

Yara Osman is a hardworking young and energetic individual serving the architecture and building industry, always looking for knowledge that advances the latest ideas in building management. Yara was both a student representative in the Atelier Student Government and a student ambassador. When she is not tutoring students of architecture, interior architecture, design studies and landscape architecture at the BAC, she is working at SGA-Boston and attending school full time. Yara is a strong advocate of the guiding principles of time, cost, and quality in any project management endeavor. Yara possesses outstanding abilities in BIM-related software beside traditional hand sketching, and believes those are critical in communicating ideas with the client. Raised by an architect and project manager who lived through the transition from blue prints to Computer Aided Architecture Design and the merger not only of CAAD and BIM but also of the traditional method of construction and 3D-printed full-scale buildings, Yara has learned the wisdom of participating in the industry with an open mind while keeping the vision of pursuing excellence through acquisition of the latest relevant knowledge. Yara can be reached via her LinkedIn account at https://www.linkedin.com/in/yara-osman-0a1436101/.

www.ingramcontent.com/pod-product-compliance
Lightning Source LLC
Chambersburg PA
CBHW071716210326
41597CB00017B/2502